Ken Baugh is well trusted for his decades of insightful teaching, practical coaching, empathetic counseling, and authentic pastoring. Now, in this wonderful new book, Ken has distilled much of his wisdom for a wider audience. I hope everyone reads this book and then buys a copy for a friend.

RICK WARREN, author of *The Purpose Driven Life*

Many believers feel stuck between a desire to live the abundant, full life that Jesus taught and the realities of personal struggles. We don't see how the one relates to the other, so we continue asking God to help us grow while "trying harder" to be better people. That just doesn't work—it leaves us more stuck and discouraged. Ken Baugh reveals the solution: a workable system in which God wants us to walk with him through grace and intimacy, bringing him our struggles and pain as we do so. Using clear, biblical teaching and the latest neuroscience, Ken will give you practical steps to come to a place where you are all God means you to be, where you walk in peace, and where you can become free of the obstacles that keep you from moving forward. Highly recommend.

JOHN TOWNSEND, PhD, *New York Times* bestselling author of the Boundaries series

I have been anticipating Ken's inspiring, gentle guide to the Christ-formation process. This new classic is such a welcomed resource, equipping us to flourish and live as a whole person, in *shalom* as God intended. May you experience great joy on the journey.

DR. CATHERINE HART WEBER, director of Flourish Center for Wellbeing at Sierra Madre, California, author of *Flourish*

Unhindered Abundance is a health-food "smoothie" for the soul. Ken Baugh has managed to blend solid cognitive neuroscience into the healthiest spiritual traditions and practices. Not only do we enjoy the flavors that changed his life and ministry, but we also taste traces of attachment love and relational life that transform identity into the sweet taste of Jesus.

JIM WILDER, author of *Renovated*

With Scripture, life experience, and insights from brain science, *Unhindered Abundance* skillfully charts the path to Christ-formation and abundant Christian living. This carefully researched and eminently practical work shows how healthy spiritual habits rewire the human brain from spiritual apathy and addictive behaviors to the Spirit-filled life we long for but often fail to achieve.

BRUCE DEMAREST, senior professor of Christian formation at Denver Seminary

Over the years, I have learned to trust those who experience the truths they teach. Ken Baugh is such a person. When he teaches that "knowing, believing, and abiding in God's love fuels Christ-formation and the abundant life," he knows this from personal experience. I want to strongly encourage you to apply the principles in this book so you, too, can experience more of the abundant life that is available through Jesus Christ.

BILL THRALL, cofounder of Trueface, coauthor of *The Ascent of a Leader* and *The Cure*

Most of us desire to hear from God but do little to minimize the noise and distraction around us long enough to learn how to listen to him. Ken reminds us that God created us for relationship with him and those around us. God is passionately pursuing us. *Unhindered Abundance* provides the opportunity to explore the availability of that deeper experience with God.

MIKE PARKINSON, director of Trinity Ranch Ministries

Ken Baugh provides a clear guide to help us get more out of life through Christ-formation. You need not be a theologian or neuroscience scholar to understand and practice his life-building techniques. Baugh does an amazing job elucidating where science and Scripture align. I began reading this book hoping that I might use it with my graduate students, but as a clarity-providing lens, Baugh helped me realize my own desperate need for restoration—so that I, too, might live more abundantly by God's design.

DAVID A. STEVENS, EdD, professor of education and neuroscience at Tabor College

Through careful exposition of biblical teaching combined with insights from psychology and neuroscience, Ken Baugh lays out a path to holistic spiritual, emotional, and relational Christlikeness. Regardless of where you find yourself on your journey, he offers pastoral and personal guidelines toward your own unhindered abundance of Christ-formation.

MICHAEL J. WILKINS, distinguished professor emeritus of New Testament language and literature at Talbot School of Theology (Biola University)

I had the privilege of ministering with Ken Baugh for two week-long retreats and saw the positive impact of this material on people serious about progressing toward spiritual maturity and conformity to the image of Christ. The book is centered in Scripture and takes God's truth seriously. It incorporates essential insights from psychology and neuroscience. *Unhindered Abundance* provides a balanced treatment of a topic that is essential for the church in these days of uncertainty and chaos.

DR. ED CURTIS, professor emeritus of Old Testament and biblical studies at Talbot School of Theology (Biola University)

Ken Baugh provides a gushing stream of insights and grace-infused disciplines from the Bible, supplemented by findings from cognitive psychology and neurology, to invite you to experience spiritual and emotional health through "Christ-formation." Along the way, he offers his own story of brokenness and life change. Open your heart to Jesus as you read, and this book will light up your brain with God's words of life.

BILL GAULTIERE, PhD, psychologist, founder of Soul Shepherding, author of *Journey of the Soul*

If you are looking for a single book to serve as your guide to greater Christ-formation, *Unhindered Abundance* would be a good choice. It blends helpful insights together and provides concrete steps for moving forward on the journey of heart-focused discipleship.

MARCUS WARNER, president of Deeper Walk International

This is a book of great encouragement, wonderful insights, and practical tools. Rooted in robust theology, it explores the role of psychology and neurology in the transformational process, offering a deeper understanding of this pathway to spiritual growth. Ken Baugh shows us how the abundant life is possible for all of us through the work and power of the Holy Spirit. I highly recommend you read it—you will be glad you did!

TOMMY HILLIKER, president of Rockbridge Seminary

UNHINDERED

RESTORING OUR SOULS IN A

RESTORING OUR SOULS IN A

ABUNDANCE

FRAGMENTED WORLD | KEN BAUGH

NavPress

A NavPress resource published in alliance
with Tyndale House Publishers

NavPress is the publishing ministry of The Navigators, an international Christian organization and leader in personal spiritual development. NavPress is committed to helping people grow spiritually and enjoy lives of meaning and hope through personal and group resources that are biblically rooted, culturally relevant, and highly practical.

For more information, visit NavPress.com.

Unhindered Abundance: Restoring Our Souls in a Fragmented World

Copyright © 2021 by Ken Baugh. All rights reserved.

A NavPress resource published in alliance with Tyndale House Publishers

NAVPRESS and the NavPress logo are registered trademarks of NavPress, The Navigators, Colorado Springs, CO. *TYNDALE* is a registered trademark of Tyndale House Ministries. Absence of ® in connection with marks of NavPress or other parties does not indicate an absence of registration of those marks.

The Team:
Don Pape, Publisher; David Zimmerman, Acquisitions Editor; Elizabeth Schroll, Copy Editor; Faceout, Designer

Cover photograph of blue sparkles copyright © Klavdiya Krinichnaya/Shutterstock. All rights reserved.

Cover photograph of torn paper copyright © Kelly Knox/Stocksy.com. All rights reserved.

Author photo taken by Ken Baugh and used with permission.

Unless otherwise indicated, all Scripture quotations are from The ESV® Bible (The Holy Bible, English Standard Version®), copyright © 2001 by Crossway, a publishing ministry of Good News Publishers. Used by permission. All rights reserved. Scripture quotations marked MSG are taken from *THE MESSAGE*, copyright © 1993, 2002, 2018 by Eugene H. Peterson. Used by permission of NavPress. All rights reserved. Represented by Tyndale House Publishers. Scripture quotations marked NIV are taken from the Holy Bible, *New International Version,*® *NIV.*® Copyright © 1973, 1978, 1984, 2011 by Biblica, Inc.® Used by permission. All rights reserved worldwide. Scripture quotations marked NLT are taken from the *Holy Bible*, New Living Translation, copyright © 1996, 2004, 2015 by Tyndale House Foundation. Used by permission of Tyndale House Publishers, Carol Stream, Illinois 60188. All rights reserved. Scripture quotations marked TLB are taken from *The Living Bible*, copyright © 1971 by Tyndale House Foundation. Used by permission of Tyndale House Publishers, Carol Stream, Illinois 60188. All rights reserved. Scripture quotations marked TPT are from The Passion Translation®. Copyright © 2017, 2018 by Passion & Fire Ministries, Inc. Used by permission. All rights reserved. ThePassionTranslation.com.

Some of the anecdotal illustrations in this book are true to life and are included with the permission of the persons involved. All other illustrations are composites of real situations, and any resemblance to people living or dead is purely coincidental.

Excerpt from *Victory Over the Darkness* by Neil Anderson, copyright © 2000, 2013, 2020. Used by permission of Bethany House Publishers, a division of Baker Publishing Group.

For information about special discounts for bulk purchases, please contact Tyndale House Publishers at csresponse@tyndale.com, or call 1-855-277-9400.

ISBN 978-1-64158-194-3

Printed in the United States of America

27	26	25	24	23	22	21
7	6	5	4	3	2	1

To my wife, Susan: Thank you for your steadfast love, patience, and encouragement throughout this book project. We have developed this material together in the crucible of ministry and life these past thirty-four years. My life with you is an intimate experience of unhindered abundance in Christ.

CONTENTS

Foreword

AN IDEA THAT DEEPLY GRIEVES ME is that some people perceive God's interaction with people as near-scoldings about our faults. It's as if God is relentlessly focused on how we're not measuring up to a standard of always doing things good Christians are supposed to do. The result is that people experience God as a demeaning "Eternal Nag," though they would never put it that way, much less say that aloud. The Christian life, at bottom, becomes one of constant striving and inevitable failure.

Ken Baugh is determined not to let this lie gain more momentum! He insists that soul restoration and mind reorientation result in unhindered abundance. Following Jesus into that good and flourishing life is a relational process that fills our loneliness. Continual conversation with God makes our life so adventurous that watching TV seems boring.

The transformation of our souls is God's creative project. And God is good at it—he progressively changes every dimension of our persons: mind, emotions, will, body, social context, and soul. Ken wisely yet gently guides us into discipleship of the mind. I say "gently" because he understands that God *woos* us into goodness. For example, Ken shares the "accidental memorization" method of learning Scripture by heart. That is how spiritual practices work. At their best, they are organic, not forced. God invites us into a Scripture passage, and we resonate so much with it that we begin to live and breathe it. Then, committing it to memory is not taxing but as luscious as eating a candy bar.

Another misconception many people have is that this growth process pits the mind and emotions against each other, as if the mind has to corner the emotions and whip them into shape. But in truth, these two aspects work together so closely that they cannot be separated. What I choose to think about gently pulls my emotions along. What I feel can lead me to talk to God about possible solutions. As I consider what I'm grateful for in this present moment (thinking), I find my face grinning (body), and in the next moment, my mood is lifted (feeling). This is not closing our eyes to facts but opening them. For gratitude is living in reality—noticing the good things happening around us that this fragmented world trains us to overlook. This marriage of mind and emotions helps us experience God's love (a theme which Ken often comes back to) as a whole-brain experience—objective and intuitive, thinking and feeling.

Such energetic discipleship of the mind leads to oneness with God. We must never be fixed on how we're doing with spiritual practices or our character transformation. Those are crucial issues, to be sure, but the focus of attention in spiritual formation is not on us; the focus of attention is on God and what the devotional masters called "union with God." We set our minds on constant companionship with God—"God with us"—and experience the oneness with God that the apostle John loved to write about (John 1:1-2; 5:17, 23; 8:58; 14:9, 23; 16:15; 17:10, 21). We experience that need-fulfilling oneness in unhindered abundance as we intermingle our thoughts with the thoughts of God.

May your mind find great joy and adventure in doing so!

Jan Johnson

author of *When the Soul Listens*

Introduction

A FEW YEARS AGO, I was feeling frustrated with the lack of spiritual growth in my life. At the time, I had been a Christian for thirty-five years and a local church[1] pastor for over twenty years, but there was still a huge gap between where I was and where I thought I should be in Christ. Truth be told, the fruit of the Spirit was woefully lacking in my life.

I struggled to love others, I lacked joy, peace, patience, and kindness, especially while driving or when I experienced any inconvenience. I caught myself engaging in dehumanizing practices—sizing up the cashiers at the grocery store, for example, to decide which could get me out the door the fastest. I'd noticed an insufficient display of goodness, faithfulness, and gentleness in my life, and an ongoing problem with anger.

As for self-control, it was pretty much out the window—especially if there was a gallon of vanilla ice cream in the freezer.

That gives you a snapshot of some of my struggles and why I was feeling so frustrated. But things have been changing.

Six years ago, I was terminated from my position as a senior pastor. The elders decided I lacked the leadership skills to take the church to the next level. This devastating experience became the catalyst for a season of unprecedented spiritual/emotional growth.[2] I felt like I had been born again, again.

This difficult season has been a personal laboratory for me to work out the principles in this book. It has produced some significant breakthroughs for me. Don't get me wrong: I'm still a work in progress. I still struggle with criticism, feelings of insecurity, and fear. I still have a few too many masks in my closet to help me present the right image in a given situation. I still struggle at times with inconsiderate drivers and get frustrated when I'm in a hurry and the line at the grocery store is too long. But I'm experiencing new freedom from spiritual/emotional conflicts that have caused problems for me throughout my life. These problems acted like barriers to my formation in Christ, but they are becoming less and less a hindrance as I put the principles found in this book into practice.

The more I study the Bible, the more I understand that God's will for my life is to become more like Jesus in his character and to experience his quality of life. The character traits of Jesus are most easily recognized as the fruit of the Spirit (Galatians 5:22-23), while Jesus' quality of life is represented by the abundant life he mentions in John 10:10: a life characterized by love, joy, peace, and hope (to name a few).

The apostle Paul refers to our formation into the image of Christ when he writes: "And we all, with unveiled face, beholding the glory of the Lord, are being transformed into the same image from one degree of glory to another. For this comes from the Lord who is the Spirit" (2 Corinthians 3:18). Scholars and spiritual leaders refer to this process variously as progressive sanctification, spiritual formation, or spiritual growth. Personally, I like the term *Christ-formation*.

What Is Christ-Formation?

Christ-formation is the overarching goal of the Christian life. It's the result of a partnership between us and the Holy Spirit and is the practical outcome of what Jesus invited people to when he called them (and us) to be his disciples.

But if you're like me, sometimes you feel like you're not making much progress in becoming like Jesus. To be honest, the whole idea of living an abundant life seems impossible. So, what's the problem?

The problem is sin—less an act of outright rebellion against God and more a desperate attempt to avoid shame and numb unresolved emotional pain with behavior that is contrary to the will of God. Regardless of why we sin, sin itself hinders the Christ-formation process because it grieves the Holy Spirit (Ephesians 4:30) and quenches his work in our lives (1 Thessalonians 5:19).

When emotional pain is allowed to linger in the heart, it can not only drive sinful behavior but also promote spiritual/emotional conflicts that distort our perception of God, self, and others, hindering our ability to experience the abundant life. Identifying and resolving these spiritual/emotional conflicts is what this book is all about. It's an interactive guide that will help you understand your direct involvement in the Holy Spirit's work to grow you in Christ. None of us will become fully formed in Christ in this life, but I believe that more transformation is possible than we realize.

What Makes This Book Unique?

The principles for Christ-formation found in this book are grounded in a robust biblical theology—but that's not necessarily new or different. What makes this book unique is its holistic approach to progressive sanctification: the lifelong process of being formed into the image of Christ. The progressive sanctification I'm laying out here is based on a robust biblical theology and infused with findings from psychology and neurology. These findings deepen our understanding about how Christ-formation works and the changes you can expect.[3] Sadly, many people think science and Scripture are at odds with each other. I believe there are points of intersection, as the regular reference to Scripture in the book will reflect.

As you study the information and apply the biblical principles in *Unhindered Abundance*, you will discover that Christ-formation is not a passive process. Like any relationship, our discipleship to Jesus is dynamic and interactive—God at work in us, and us participating in that work with God. Neither does Christ-formation happen in isolation; you need to join with others on the same journey. So I encourage you to work through this material with a friend or in a small group. (At the end of each chapter, you will find questions for personal reflection and questions you can use with a small group.)

This material has been forged in the fires of my own life experiences. You will find some chapters fairly rigorous as we explore and apply findings from theology, psychology, and neurology to our understanding of Christ-formation, but I promise I will walk you through the practical implications, step by step.

My greatest desire is that this book will help you identify and resolve the spiritual/emotional conflicts that have hindered your Christ-formation so that you will experience a greater degree of the abundant life that Jesus has made possible for you.

1

DEFINING THE DISCIPLESHIP PROBLEM

IN A WORLD INFECTED WITH SIN, emotional pain is a universal human reality. Whether this pain is self-inflicted due to poor choices or it comes at the hands of other people or through difficult circumstances, emotional pain is real and can be as debilitating as physical pain. Allowed to linger in the heart, emotional pain will often produce additional issues, such as depression, anxiety, loneliness, fear, anger, unforgiveness, and a range of other problems that can wreak havoc in our lives.

Many believers in Christ attempt to numb their emotional pain through sinful behavior and addictions. These responses create barriers to transformation. Whether we sin or are sinned against, the spiritual/emotional conflicts sin produces keep us stuck and hinder our ability to experience the abundant life available in Christ.

The Greatest Barrier to Spiritual Growth

I have been shocked to discover the large number of Christians who feel stuck in their spiritual growth as a result of sin and unresolved emotional pain. About a decade ago, Willow Creek Community Church in South Barrington,

Illinois, conducted a survey of their congregation. By 2015, the *Reveal* study had been administered in approximately two thousand churches, including an estimated 425,000 participants.[1] The findings were alarming:

- Of the people surveyed, 16 percent described the condition of their spiritual lives as stalled or unsatisfying.

- Additionally, 27 percent of those surveyed confessed to a variety of addictions, including overspending, gambling, excessive drinking of alcohol, pornography, and overeating.

- Another 16 percent of those surveyed admitted to having affairs or inappropriate relationships that pulled them away from God.

- Another 48 percent admitted to struggling with emotional issues, such as depression, anger, and suppressing painful emotions.

- A total of 89 percent of those surveyed acknowledged that they were not making their spiritual growth a priority.[2]

These findings present a very real problem that is not being addressed by traditional means of discipleship: Bible study, prayer, small-group participation, church programs, Christian service, and financial generosity. There is more Bible-study curriculum available today than ever before, more books pertaining to spiritual formation and growth, more biblical teaching available on Facebook Live, Vimeo, and YouTube, and an ever-increasing number of excellent Christian podcasts. Yet large numbers of believers confess to being stuck in addiction and behaviors that hinder their growth in Christ. The vast amount of good biblical *information* is not facilitating much in the way of *transformation*.

To put it simply, the great barrier to spiritual growth among many Christians living in North America is due to *unresolved emotional pain*.

In order to address this problem, we need to understand how spiritual growth and emotional health influence each other. We need a more holistic and biblical understanding of the heart—one's inner being, composed of thought, emotion, and will—to discover how unresolved emotional pain contributes to the spiritual/emotional conflicts that hinder the transformation process. Until we develop a more whole-hearted approach to discipleship, we will continue to perpetuate the problem.

Maybe you're aware of a gap between where you are and where you think you should be in your life as a Christian. I've been a Christian for over forty years and a pastor for twenty-seven years. I have advanced degrees in theology. And yet I still struggle spiritually and emotionally. I can assure you that these problems are not due to a lack of biblical knowledge, spiritual-growth practices, or a desire to be a godly man. As with so many of us, the barrier to my growth in Christ is unresolved emotional pain.

My Story

When I was five years old, my parents divorced. Of course, it was never their intention to cause me harm—my parents loved me and did the best they could in a very difficult situation. However, I'm tenderhearted by nature, and following their divorce, I experienced intense feelings of rejection, abandonment, and fear. These feelings promoted spiritual/emotional conflicts that distorted my perception of God, myself, and others. They were held together by a deep sense of shame.

My feelings of rejection, abandonment, fear, and shame increased during my early adolescent years. I struggled to fit in with other kids at school, and my insecurities made me an easy target for bullies. My neediness and hunger for adult approval was annoying to my teachers.

A few years after my parents divorced, they each remarried. My stepmother was kind and nurturing, but my stepfather, while being a good provider and husband to my mother, was stern and emotionally unavailable. His gruff impatience only contributed to my feelings of rejection, abandonment, fear, and shame.

When I was twelve, my mother and stepfather sent me from California to Utah to live on their ranch with my grandparents. This was meant to be temporary while my stepfather waited for a job transfer to a new power plant under construction, but the approval process dragged on and the project was eventually canceled. I ended up living with my grandparents in Utah for three years. While I'm grateful that during that time I became a Christian (I responded to an invitation given by Billy Graham during one of his TV crusades), my emotional turmoil continued as I struggled with my peers in school.

My classmates didn't take kindly to the new kid from California. I was teased and physically bullied incessantly. No matter what I did, I just couldn't fit in; there was no place where I felt like I belonged. I only had two friends, but even they were reluctant to eat with me during lunch or sit with me on the bus ride to and from school. Most of the time, I just sat by myself feeling sad and alone. I was experiencing extreme anxiety from being separated from my mother, and the emotional hurt I experienced from the kids at school reinforced my feelings of rejection, abandonment, fear, and shame. My grandparents did the best they could to love and console me, but it just wasn't enough to ease my emotional trauma.

I moved back to Southern California to live with my mother and stepfather while I attended high school. I was good at basketball, and I made the summer league team before my freshman year. The coach replaced one of the starting players with me, which I thought would help me be accepted by my peers and find a place to belong. Sadly, it didn't turn out that way: Most of the guys on the freshman team resented the fact that the coach played me more than their longtime friend. This situation intensified my feelings of rejection, abandonment, fear, and shame; these feelings seemed to follow me everywhere.

After graduating from high school, I lied about my age and took up bartending. For the next three years, I tended bar for yacht parties, corporate functions, and banquets at a gourmet restaurant near where I lived. During these years, I numbed my emotional pain with alcohol and sex, but any brief experience of relief was followed quickly by more guilt and shame. As a believer, I was in turmoil about my behavior; I knew without a doubt that what I was doing was wrong, but I wanted to numb my pain. I can remember times when I clearly sensed God's loving presence and the invitation to turn away from my life of sin, but to no avail. I was stuck in a relentless cycle of sin and sorrow.

After a few years, my world came crashing down on me. The woman I was living with came home one night and told me she had just had an abortion. It seemed like a matter-of-fact decision for her, but I was devastated. The pain of the abortion drove us apart, and not long after, we split up, bringing my feelings of rejection, abandonment, fear, and shame to a tipping point.

One day I was walking alone on the beach, feeling a great sense of despair as I thought about how I had made such a mess of my life. I literally fell to my knees and cried out to God for help and forgiveness. It felt in that moment like God lowered a rope to help me out of my pit of despair. I recommitted my life to following Jesus and began my journey to becoming a pastor.

As I look back today, I realize that the mess I had made of my life had less to do with a hard and rebellious heart and more to do with a broken heart—damaged by years of emotional pain that fostered an intense longing to be loved. Obviously I had made sinful choices for which I was responsible, and those choices had produced grave consequences. Sinful choices are always a matter of free will, but they may be influenced by unresolved emotional pain and distorted thinking. They may be motivated by shame. Shame distorts your identity and undermines your sense of value as a person created in the image of God. People who live with deep shame feel defective and unworthy of love.

I am grateful for God's mercy in my life. But even though God forgave my sin, he did not remove my distorted thinking nor the spiritual/emotional conflicts that followed me from my youth. Those feelings of rejection, abandonment, fear, and shame would not be addressed until years later, when I learned about Christ-formation.

What Is Christ-Formation?

In 2 Corinthians 3:18, Paul writes, "We all, with unveiled face, beholding the glory of the Lord, are being transformed into the same image from one degree of glory to another. For this comes from the Lord who is the Spirit." Some scholars and church leaders refer to this process of transformation as progressive sanctification. Others describe it as spiritual formation, spiritual growth, or spiritual maturity. I prefer to use the term *Christ-formation* because it is more descriptive of what is taking place: We are becoming more like Christ.

To become more like Jesus Christ includes two lifelong experiences. First, it involves taking on facets of his character that are most easily identified as the fruit of the Spirit: "love, joy, peace, patience, kindness, goodness, faithfulness, gentleness, self-control" (Galatians 5:22-23). It's important to recognize that the fruit of the Spirit is singular, not plural. The first fruit of the Spirit is love; the by-product of this love is joy, peace, patience, kindness, goodness, faithfulness, gentleness, and self-control.

This understanding of love as the fruit of the Spirit takes us to the second experience of Christ-formation: the abundant life. As we internalize the reality of God's love in increasing measure, we will begin to experience a different quality of life—a life characterized by joy, peace, patience, kindness, goodness, faithfulness, gentleness, and self-control. This is the abundant life. The more we abide in Jesus' love, the more like Jesus we will become and the more we will experience the abundant life.

In the next chapter, we will look at qualities of the abundant life and the lies that keep us from experiencing it.

Restoring My Soul with God

1. How have you seen unresolved emotional pain hinder spiritual growth in others? How have you seen it affect your growth?

_____

_____

_____

2. In your own words, write out the problem this creates for following Christ:

_____

_____

_____

3. Circle all the emotions you have experienced in your life from the list below:

Rejected	Abandoned	Sad	Lonely	Fearful
Depressed	Unpopular	Envious	Resentful	Hateful
Angry	Regretful	Spiteful	Disappointed	Devastated
Inadequate	Helpless	Shamed	Hopeless	Guilty
Worthless	Humiliated	Threatened	Shocked	Trapped
Terrified	Tense	Tempted	Anxious	Furious

4. Pair the above feelings to the situation that caused them and write out what happened as best as you can remember. Be as specific as possible: How old you were at the time, names of the people involved, where the situation occurred, who you have shared this experience with. Use a journal if needed.

_____

_____

_____

5. On a separate sheet of paper, make a list of all the major life events (positive and negative) you can remember under the age categories below:

0–5 years old	6–10 years old	11–20 years old
21–30 years old	31–40 years old	41–50 years old
51–60 years old	61–70 years old	71–80 years old
80+		

Restoring My Soul with Others

1. Does it surprise you that there is little statistical difference in the daily lives of believers and unbelievers? Why do you think so many believers continue to struggle with addictions?

2. In keeping with the _Reveal_ study referred to in this chapter, how do church programs help and hinder the Christ-formation process?

3. How do you think emotional health contributes to spiritual growth?

4. How would you describe the Christ-formation process? What is the goal of Christ-formation? How long does it take? How does it take place?

5. As you think about your own painful life experiences, how have they helped or hindered your Christ-formation process?

2

THE ABUNDANT LIFE

WHEN I WAS A LITTLE BOY, I had a picture of Jesus in my room. He was leaning on a shepherd's staff, watching over a flock of sheep. I remember this picture well: The meadow was lush and green, the sun was bright, the sky was deep blue, and the look on Jesus' face was serene but alert.

This picture would remind me that Jesus is the Good Shepherd, always looking out for his sheep. That's good news, because a good shepherd *must* be alert, constantly protecting the sheep against predators. Based on my experience with sheep while living on my family's ranch in Utah, sheep can't protect themselves: They are some of the most helpless animals you will ever find.

Sheep don't have claws or sharp teeth. They certainly are not known for their speed and agility. Sheep are, consequently, easy targets for hungry predators.

Not only are sheep unable to protect themselves, they are prone to wander and often get into trouble. If one sheep gets its head through a hole in the fence to reach some grass on the other side, it won't be long before he makes the hole large enough to squeeze his entire body through. And once one gets through, it's only a matter of time before the whole flock follows. Inevitably a few sheep will get tangled up in the now broken-down fence, and as they struggle to get free of the barbed wire, they can get badly cut. Bleeding sheep are in serious danger because predators can smell blood from far away.

When Jesus likens us, as his followers, to sheep, he isn't exactly giving us a compliment. And yet, Jesus is the consummate Good Shepherd. Regardless of the trouble we cause him, he lovingly provides us with a quality of life that he describes as abundant.

What Did Jesus Mean by the Abundant Life?

I used to resist the biblical concept of the abundant life, which Jesus refers to in John 10:10. For some reason, I associated it with a version of the gospel that promises health and wealth as outcomes of salvation. I thought that the abundant life was largely reserved for eternity in heaven. However, Jesus clearly said, "I came that they may have life and have it abundantly." His words here describe an ongoing, present-tense reality available to every Christian right here and right now.

I have come to believe that the abundant life to which Jesus is referring is a quality of life that emanates as we immerse ourselves in the reality of God's love and experience greater intimacy with Jesus. When we do this, we will thrive—regardless of our circumstances. New Testament scholar D. A. Carson maintains that Jesus' reference to the abundant life "suggests fat, contented, flourishing sheep, not terrorized by brigands [robbers]. . . . The life Jesus' true disciples enjoy is not to be construed as more time to fill (merely 'everlasting' life), but life at its scarcely imagined best, life to be lived."[1] God's love produces an inner condition in the heart that is captured in the Hebrew word *shalom*.

Shalom refers to an inner state of completeness, wholeness, and tranquility. If you were in Israel and someone said "Shalom" to you, they would be saying something like "May your life be full of well-being." Shalom refers to a quality of life that is accessible only through a relationship with the Lord. The Aaronic, or high priestly, blessing in Numbers 6:23-26 captures the essence of shalom: "The LORD bless you and keep you; the LORD make his face to shine upon you and be gracious to you; the LORD lift up his countenance upon you and give you peace." This prayer is a good reminder of God's nature and character, especially as it relates to his people.

A core attribute of God's nature is love (1 John 4:8), which is visible through his generous provision and gracious loving care for his people. God looks on his people with favor and great affection, and he is always present and willing to provide for our needs. We find evidence for God's loving nature and character throughout the Bible. For example, God described himself to Moses saying, "The LORD, the LORD, a God merciful and gracious, slow to anger, and abounding in steadfast love and faithfulness" (Exodus 34:6). David describes God in Psalm 103:8 as "compassionate and merciful, slow to get angry and filled with unfailing love" (NLT). Jesus referred to God as our "heavenly Father" who provides for the birds and the grass of the fields so richly that we—as his children—don't need to worry about a thing because God loves us even more than them (Matthew 6:25-30). We can be confident in all this because God's character is empowered by his divine nature.

God alone is all-powerful, all-present, and all-knowing. Consequently, when God's people think rightly about him, they will experience peace. Isaiah writes, "You will keep in perfect peace all who trust in you, *all whose thoughts are fixed on you*" (Isaiah 26:3, NLT, emphasis added). The Hebrew word Isaiah uses for "peace" is *shalom*. Therefore, the life of shalom that Jesus, the Good Shepherd, makes available for his sheep is a life blessed with God's presence, protection, and provision—a life characterized by a growing capacity to know and experience God's love.

Sadly, in my experience, very few believers experience the degree of the abundant life that is available to them in Christ. Why? Because believers are engaged in a spiritual battle with Satan and his demonic horde.

The Battle for Shalom

Prior to Jesus' statement about the abundant life in John 10:10, he says that Satan is a "thief [who] comes only to steal and kill and destroy." Jesus is pointing out that Satan will do everything he can to keep you as a believer from experiencing a life of shalom. How? By tempting you to believe his lies. Satan is the great deceiver, and deception is his primary weapon. He tempted Eve in the Garden with lies (Genesis 3:1-4); he unsuccessfully tempted Jesus in the wilderness with lies (Matthew 4:1-11); and today, Satan is attempting to deceive the whole world with lies (Revelation 12:9). The battle for shalom is spiritual warfare—it is fought and won on the battlefield of your mind, in your thoughts.

The apostle Paul writes in Ephesians 6:10-12 that every believer is engaged in a spiritual battle with Satan and his minions:

Finally, be strong in the Lord and in the strength of his might. Put on the whole armor of God, that you may be able to stand against the schemes of the devil. For we do not wrestle against flesh and blood, but against the rulers, against the authorities, against the cosmic powers over this present darkness, against the spiritual forces of evil in the heavenly places.

It is important to remember that Jesus has conquered the devil and his army of fallen angels (Colossians 2:15), but it is also true that Satan is still active in this world. Peter writes, "Your adversary the devil prowls around like a roaring lion, seeking someone to devour" (1 Peter 5:8). Satan attempts to devour believers through deception infused with shame and fear. Jesus summed up Satan's character by saying, "He has always hated the truth, because there is no truth in him. When he lies, it is consistent with his character; for he is a liar and the father of lies" (John 8:44, NLT). Therefore, the spiritual battle believers are fighting is on the battlefield of the mind, combating Satan's lies with God's truth.

The most effective way to fight against these lies is to compare them to God's truth as revealed in the Bible. Paul refers to this tactic as taking your thoughts captive to Christ:

The weapons of our warfare are not of the flesh but have divine power to destroy strongholds. We destroy arguments and every lofty opinion raised against the knowledge of God, and take every thought captive to obey Christ.

2 CORINTHIANS 10:4-5

Comparing Satan's lies to God's truth in the Bible will prevent them from taking root and becoming a stronghold in your mind.

How to Identify Satan's Lies

In order to fight effectively, we must first identify the lie: You can't fight something you can't see. But Satan's lies are easy to spot. Satan will attempt to deceive you into believing lies about God, yourself, and other people. These lies often promote spiritual/emotional conflicts and emotions (including shame and fear) that hinder the ability to experience the life of shalom.

Psychologists Wilkie Au and Noreen Canon Au write, "Shame is rooted in a deep-seated fear that we are flawed, inadequate, and unworthy of love."[2] Consequently, shame is one of Satan's most destructive weapons: It produces fear and leads to isolation, where our vulnerability to his lies compounds. Let's take a closer look at each type of lie that Satan will tempt you to believe.

Satan's Lies about God

Satan will tempt you to believe that God is against you. In truth, God is for you. Paul writes, "If God is for us, who can be against us?" (Romans 8:31).

Another lie Satan wants you to believe is that God is disappointed in you. The truth is "there is therefore now no condemnation for those who are in Christ Jesus" (Romans 8:1).

Satan wants you to believe that God has more important things to deal with than you and your problems. But God is deeply concerned about you and knows everything that is going on in your life. In fact, God knows the number of hairs on your head (Luke 12:7) and has captured every tear in his bottle (Psalm 56:8).

Satan will tempt you to believe that your sin is the exception to God's forgiveness. And yet, the Bible is clear that Jesus paid the price for all sin—including your sin and mine—when he died on the cross. When he cried out, "It is finished" (John 19:30), he was declaring, in part, that the penalty for sin—past, present, and future—is paid in full. Paul writes, "When he was hung on the cross, he took upon himself the curse for our wrongdoing" (Galatians 3:13, NLT). In fact, God promises that when you confess your sin, he will always forgive you (1 John 1:9). God will never turn away from a broken and contrite heart (Psalm 51:17).

Satan's Lies about You

Satan would love nothing more than for you to see yourself as a dirty, rotten sinner. But this is a lie. The truth is, at the moment of salvation, God no longer refers to you as a sinner but as a saint.

Paul regularly addresses his letters to saints: "the saints who are in Ephesus" (Ephesians 1:1); "all the saints in Christ Jesus who are at Philippi" (Philippians 1:1); "the saints and faithful brothers in Christ at Colossae" (Colossians 1:2). Other early leaders of the church understood followers of

Jesus to be saints: Ananias expressed his concern to God about approaching Saul by saying, "I have heard from many about this man, how much evil he has done to your saints at Jerusalem" (Acts 9:13). Peter went to visit the "saints who lived at Lydda" (Acts 9:32). In fact, the word *saint* is used sixty-one times in the King James Version of the Bible to refer to believers.

This is a powerful witness to the new identity we have in Christ. And yet, I have found that a lot of believers resist the designation. Many think that to be a "saint" means you have to live a sin-free life. But that's not the case at all. It is true that Christians sin (1 John 1:8). Nevertheless, Christians are saints. The difference between a sinner and a saint is not that one continues to sin while the other does not, but that one is enslaved to sin while the other is not. To be a believer is to be graced with the choice whether to sin or not.

In Christ, we are now dead to sin and slaves to righteousness: "We know that our old self was crucified with him in order that the body of sin might be brought to nothing, so that we would no longer be enslaved to sin. For one who has died has been set free from sin" (Romans 6:6-7). At the moment of salvation, every believer becomes a new creation in Christ (2 Corinthians 5:17), with a new heart with new and right desires (Ezekiel 36:26). In Christ, every believer becomes a child of God (John 1:12), a brother or sister to Jesus (Romans 8:29), and a coheir with Christ (Romans 8:17). The truth about you is that God has clothed you in the righteousness of Christ (2 Corinthians 5:21).

The devil will tempt you to believe that when you choose to sin, you show that you are still a slave to sin and thus unworthy of God's love. And yet, God's truth reveals just the opposite: God's love for us is based not on our worthiness but on the exercise of his nature to love.

God created you in his image and likeness (Genesis 1:27); therefore, you have value. God delights in his people: "He will take delight in you with gladness. . . . He will rejoice over you with joyful songs" (Zephaniah 3:17, NLT). The Bible declares that he has written the names of his people on the palm of his hand (Isaiah 49:16). God is deeply concerned about the well-being of his people, including you.

This might be the most amazing truth of all: God the Father loves you as much as he loves Jesus, his Son. Look carefully at Jesus' words in his High Priestly Prayer:

I have given them the glory that you gave me, that they may be one as we are one—I in them and you in me—so that they may be brought to complete unity. Then the world will know that you sent me and have loved them even as you have loved me. . . . I have made you known to them, and will continue to make you known in order that the love you have for me may be in them and that I myself may be in them.

JOHN 17:22-23, 26, NIV

The fact that God the Father loves every believer with the same love that he has for Jesus is astounding. New Testament scholar Craig Keener writes, "That the Father loved Jesus' disciples 'even as' (καθὼς) he loved Jesus ([John] 17:23) is one of the most remarkable statements of the Gospel, given the enormity of God's love for his uniquely obedient Son."[3] You can have every confidence that God loves you with a consistent, everlasting love.[4] The light of God's Word exposes the darkness of Satan's lies, making them easy to see.

Here is the truth about sin. At the moment of salvation, you are forgiven the penalty for your sin (Romans 3:23-24), you are free from any and all condemnation (Romans 8:1), and you are spared from the wrath of God forever (Romans 5:9; 1 Thessalonians 5:9). In Christ, you are God's beloved son or daughter (Galatians 3:26), one in whom Christ dwells (Galatians 2:20), and one for whom God has ordained every day of your life (Psalm 139:16). As a child of God, you have no need to worry or fret about the future. Jesus said that God the Father cares for the birds of the air and the flowers of the field, but he cares even more for you (Matthew 6:26-34). In fact, Jesus invites you to live free of worry (Matthew 6:31-34), and Peter says you can cast all your anxiety on him (1 Peter 5:7).

Satan wants you to believe that there is no one who really cares about you, that you are alone, and that the only person you can rely on is yourself. This, too, is a lie. The truth is that Jesus' Spirit, the Holy Spirit, lives in your heart (Romans 8:11), and Jesus promised that he would never leave you (Matthew 28:20).

These lies of Satan and the corresponding truths from God's Word are only a small sample found in the Bible, but they show you how to identify lies about yourself and replace them with God's truth.

Satan's Lies about Others

The third type of lie Satan will tempt you to believe are lies about other people. One of those lies is that you cannot trust anyone: People will always hurt you. It's true, there are many people in your life who have hurt you and whom you cannot trust. But it's not true of everyone.

In the Bible, we find a number of close, reliable friendships: Moses had Aaron, Elijah had Elisha, Naomi had Ruth, David had Jonathan, Jesus had his disciples, Paul had Timothy. These biblical friendships show us that there are people who are willing to carry your burdens (Galatians 6:2), people who will accept you for who you are (Romans 15:7), people who will cry with you when you are sad (Romans 12:15), and people who will help you up when you are down (2 Timothy 4:13).

I'm not suggesting that great friendships are easy to find or that your closest friend will never hurt you at some point, but people need people. Be discerning, but be careful you don't buy into the lie that you are alone in this world and there is nobody you can trust.

I have a number of safe people in my life in whom I can confide, including my wife, Susan. These people have demonstrated over time that they can be trusted. There is always the risk of getting hurt, even by the people you love and trust the most, but it's a risk you need to take because God wired you for love: You cannot thrive alone. Over the years, I have been hurt by people close to me, but I have discovered that my reluctance to trust others is often more about my own pride—not wanting to appear weak or make myself vulnerable—than about their trustworthiness.

Here is a rule of thumb that has served me well: Be the kind of friend you want to have. I think that's good advice.

Don't Fear the Toothless Lion

In this chapter, we have looked at the stark contrast between Jesus, the Good Shepherd who cares for his flock, and Satan, a predator ready to pounce on his prey. Satan and his minions will tempt you to believe lies about God, yourself, and others, but you can choose to take those thoughts captive and replace the lies with God's truth. Don't forget, the devil has been defeated by the Lord Jesus (Hebrews 2:14) and has no power or authority over you; all he can do is attempt to deceive and intimidate you.

Each October, the theme of an amusement park near where I live in

Southern California changes from Knott's Berry Farm to Knott's Scary Farm: The entire park is turned into a ghoulish Halloween nightmare. The cast members dress up in the scariest costumes you can imagine—the kind of stuff you see in a Hollywood horror film. There is only one rule that each cast member must follow, no matter what: They cannot touch a guest. They can get right up in your face, they can get as close as their breath, but they can't physically touch you.

This cast of terrifying creatures can pretend they are going to cut you down with a chainsaw or drag you off into a dungeon to be tortured, but that's all they are allowed to do, to scare you. The same is true of your enemy, the devil; he is a toothless lion.

Don't get me wrong, Satan can be very convincing and intimidating: He exists as a very powerful fallen angel, but all he can do is scare you and tempt you with his lies. You can prevail.[5] The Bible contains all the truth—the very words of God—you need to tear down any stronghold in your mind (2 Corinthians 10:4-5). Jesus Christ, your Lord, Savior, brother, and friend, is the creator and sustainer of all things: "By him all things were created, in heaven and on earth, visible and invisible, whether thrones or dominions or rulers or authorities—all things were created through him and for him. And he is before all things, and in him all things hold together" (Colossians 1:16-17). The King of kings and the Lord of lords (Revelation 19:16), Jesus has all power and authority over Satan and his entire army of fallen angels (Matthew 28:18). There is nothing and no one who can separate you from God's love or change your identity as his son or daughter. I find tremendous encouragement in Paul's words to the Romans:

> So, what do you think? With God on our side like this, how can
> we lose? If God didn't hesitate to put everything on the line for
> us, embracing our condition and exposing himself to the worst
> by sending his own Son, is there anything else he wouldn't gladly
> and freely do for us? And who would dare tangle with God by
> messing with one of God's chosen? Who would dare even to
> point a finger? The One who died for us—who was raised to life
> for us!—is in the presence of God at this very moment sticking up
> for us. Do you think anyone is going to be able to drive a wedge

between us and Christ's love for us? There is no way! Not trouble, not hard times, not hatred, not hunger, not homelessness, not bullying threats, not backstabbing, not even the worst sins listed in Scripture:

> They kill us in cold blood because they hate you.
> We're sitting ducks; they pick us off one by one.

None of this fazes us because Jesus loves us. I'm absolutely convinced that nothing—nothing living or dead, angelic or demonic, today or tomorrow, high or low, thinkable or unthinkable—absolutely *nothing* can get between us and God's love because of the way that Jesus our Master has embraced us.

ROMANS 8:31-39, MSG

You can rest in the fact that you belong to the Lord and are sealed by the Holy Spirit (2 Corinthians 1:22; 5:5; Ephesians 1:13-14; 4:30). Remember, Jesus paid the price for sin by dying on a cross; the moment you put your faith in him and his sacrifice for your sin, you are born again and become a new person in Christ, adopted into the family of God (Romans 8:15; Galatians 4:5) with all the rights and privileges of a beloved son or daughter. Paul writes, "The Spirit himself bears witness with our spirit that we are children of God, and if children, then heirs—heirs of God and fellow heirs with Christ" (Romans 8:16-17). You are God's beloved (Colossians 3:12), and Jesus—your Savior, Lord, Friend, Brother, and Good Shepherd—has secured for you an eternal home in heaven (John 14:2). He also offers you an abundant life here on Earth—a life of shalom.

Whether or not you experience this life of shalom is your choice. God loves you so much that he will not demand or coerce you to experience it. Neither will he condemn you if you don't claim what is yours in Christ. But he has made it available to you.

The question is, how will you choose to respond? Will you embrace a life of shalom or stay stuck in the muck of spiritual/emotional conflicts promoted by Satan's lies?

Below is a chart to summarize what you have read in this chapter; it reveals the contrast between Jesus as the Good Shepherd and Satan as the Father of Lies.

JESUS THE GOOD SHEPHERD	SATAN THE FATHER OF LIES
REST	EXHAUSTION
PROVISION	SCARCITY
HELP	HURT
RESTORE	DESTROY
LOVE	FEAR
POSITIVE	NEGATIVE
HOPE	DESPAIR
RELATIONSHIP	ISOLATION
PEACE	WORRY
CONFIDENCE	INSECURITY
JOY	SORROW
FORGIVENESS	CONDEMNATION
LIFE	DEATH
FRIEND	FOE
TRUTH	LIES

Now, you might be wondering how this Christ-formation process works. That's what this book is all about, so let's begin the process of discovery. In the next chapter, I will describe in detail three essential ingredients for the Christ-formation process. These ingredients provide the foundation for how the growth and change process works practically.

Restoring My Soul with God

The following exercises are meant to be done over the course of five days.

1. Read Colossians 1:15-17. Write down the words that describe Jesus. How do these words describe Jesus' ability to protect you from Satan?

_____

_____

_____

2. Read Ephesians 6:10-19. What stands out to you from this passage? What do you learn about God? What do you learn about your adversary?

_____

_____

_____

3. Read through the list of Satan's lies on pages 17–20. Summarize the lies in as few words as possible. Then, take those lies captive to Christ (2 Corinthians 10:4-6) by answering the following questions for each: *What is the lie?* and *What does God say is the truth?*

_____

_____

_____

4. Write out the verses you chose to replace Satan's lies with (see question 3) on 3 × 5 cards. Plan to review them in the morning and evening for thirty days. This will replace Satan's lies with God's truth and help you experience shalom.

5. Begin the thirty-day process of reviewing your 3 × 5 cards.

Restoring My Soul with Others

1. How have you thought about the abundant life before? How would you describe it to someone now?

2. Read John 10:1-10 together. What traits do you see in the passage that describe Jesus as the Good Shepherd? What is Jesus' desire for his sheep?

3. Discuss the contrast between Jesus and Satan from the chart on page 23. What stands out to you the most about Jesus' desires for you and Satan's desires for you?

4. Review the list of Scriptures in Appendix D. Of the three types of satanic lies—about God, yourself, and others—which ones do you struggle with the most? Which verses help you the most to stand firm against Satan's schemes?

3

INGREDIENTS FOR CHRIST-FORMATION

IN 2010, I WAS STANDING AT the finish line of the Los Angeles Marathon, waiting to cheer for my oldest daughter as she completed her race. I remember watching the runners and thinking how normal they all looked (well, at least most of them looked normal—there was the occasional runner wearing a gorilla mask or tutu or dribbling a basketball while running barefoot). For the most part, the runners I saw were not eccentrics, nor were they elite athletes: They were normal people like me.

I remember thinking, *I could do this. It can't be that hard.* I decided right then and there that I was going to run the LA Marathon the following year. And I did! I actually ran 26.2 miles, all the way from Dodger Stadium to the Santa Monica Pier—in the pouring rain and freezing cold, no less.

The reason I finished the race was not because I tried really hard but because I trained really smart. There is a huge difference between trying and training.[1]

I knew if I was going to succeed at the marathon, I would need help, so I found a trainer. She mapped out the number of miles I needed to run each week (on average, I ran thirty-eight miles per week for twenty weeks), and she also advised me on what to eat and how much rest I needed between runs. She even helped me buy the right type of shoes and running gear. I learned a lot about running, and I trained hard during the months before the marathon.

You can imagine how good it felt when I crossed the finish line on race day. Actually, I burst out crying, I was so glad it was over. Those last few miles of the marathon had been absolute agony—I was in so much pain I just wanted to run into oncoming traffic and get it over with. But I pushed through the pain and the mental anguish, and because I had trained smart, I had developed the mental and physical ability to run 26.2 miles.

Now, imagine the outcome if one day I had said to my wife, Susan, "You know what, honey? I'm going to run the LA Marathon tomorrow. I know I've never run that far before, and I haven't done any training. But I'm going to try really, really hard." If that's all I did to prepare, how far do you think I could have run on race day? Not very far, right? Why? Because I hadn't trained myself to run 26.2 miles. The truth is, no amount of willpower would have made any difference—without proper training, I would have failed to finish the race.

My training routine wasn't complicated, but it did involve an intentional process composed of three ingredients: information, relationships, and direct interaction. These same three ingredients facilitate the Christ-formation process.

Three Ingredients for Christ-Formation

In order to finish the marathon, I needed the right *information*. I needed to learn how to run 26.2 miles. I needed to know what clothing and shoes to buy and which supplements to take. This information was essential to my goal.

I also needed the right *relationships*. I needed a trainer who had marathon experience and knew how to train me. I needed the support of my wife and family—training for a marathon would take a lot of time away from them. Additionally, I needed the help of a chiropractor: You can't imagine the pounding that your body takes when running close to forty miles a week. These relationships were essential to my goal.

Finally, I needed to *exert personal effort*. Nobody else could train for me. Nobody else could eat the right food and rest my body between runs. These are things that only I could do. My own participation in this process was essential to my goal.

None of these three ingredients alone—information, relationships, direct participation—would have been sufficient to accomplish my goal. But when they were combined, I had everything I needed to finish the race. The process of Christ-formation is different from running a marathon, but the same three ingredients apply to both. Let me show you what I mean.

Ingredient #1: Information

Divine revelation provides the information essential to Christ-formation. God's revelation comes to us in two forms: special and general. Special revelation refers to what is revealed in Scripture. Paul writes,

> All Scripture is inspired by God and is useful to teach us what is
> true and to make us realize what is wrong in our lives. It corrects
> us when we are wrong and teaches us to do what is right. God uses
> it to prepare and equip his people to do every good work.
> 2 TIMOTHY 3:16-17, NLT

The Bible is God's special revelation because it contains the very words of God, directed by the Holy Spirt and written down by the prophets and apostles. Peter writes,

> No prophecy of Scripture is a matter of private opinion. And
> why? Because it's not something concocted in the human heart.
> Prophecy resulted when the Holy Spirit prompted men and
> women to speak God's Word.
> 2 PETER 1:20-21, MSG

The essential information about Christ-formation found in the Bible cannot be found anywhere else. How can you learn that God is loving and personal (Revelation 3:20) without the Bible? How can you know that you need a Savior (John 3:16-17) or that Jesus Christ is that Savior, the only one who could pay the price for your sin (Hebrews 9:12-14), without the Bible?

Without the Bible, you can't know that God is three equal yet distinct divine persons—Father, Son, and Holy Spirit (1 Peter 1:1-2). You cannot learn about your identity in Christ.[2] The volume of information for

Christ-formation that is unique to the Bible is immense. And yet, the Bible isn't the only source of such essential information.

General revelation is what is revealed in creation about God and his desires for the world: "His invisible attributes, namely, his eternal power and divine nature, have been clearly perceived, ever since the creation of the world, in the things that have been made" (Romans 1:20). David refers to God's general revelation in Psalm 19:1-2: "The heavens declare the glory of God, and the sky above proclaims his handiwork. Day to day pours out speech, and night to night reveals knowledge."

A great deal can be learned about God and Christ-formation by observing creation. For example, we can learn things about God from animals, birds, and even fish: "Just ask the animals, and they will teach you. Ask the birds of the sky, and they will tell you. Speak to the earth, and it will instruct you. Let the fish in the sea speak to you" (Job 12:7-8, NLT). King Solomon said that we can even learn life lessons by observing the ant: "Go to the ant, you sluggard; consider its ways and be wise! It has no commander, no overseer or ruler, yet it stores its provisions in summer and gathers its food at harvest" (Proverbs 6:6-8, NIV). Jesus suggested that we can resist worry and trust in the Father's provision by observing how he cares for the birds and flowers (Matthew 6:26-31).

General revelation can also be found by using the scientific method.[3] Careful study of psychology, neurology, biology, philosophy, sociology, and anthropology, to name a few, uncovers important truths about us and our world that can inform and clarify the Christ-formation process. For example, we learn from psychology how denied trauma and emotional pain can lead to spiritual/emotional conflicts that hinder growth and change. Additionally, we learn from neuroscience how to rewire our own brain, replacing negative and distorted thoughts about God, self, and others with truth derived from Scripture. Such insights help us identify things that hinder our growth and things that support the change God desires for every believer.

As important as God's revelation is, information is only the first ingredient in Christ-formation. The second is relationships.

Ingredient #2: Relationships

God is relational. He has existed for all eternity in the triune community of Father, Son, and Holy Spirit. According to the Bible, God created human beings in his image (Genesis 1:26-27). This means, among other things, that people are also relational beings: We are created for a relationship with God through Jesus Christ and with other human beings—especially other believers. Christ-formation is dependent on these relationships.

At the moment of salvation, one of the many changes that takes place in your life is that the Holy Spirit takes up residence in your heart, beginning the process of Christ-formation. Your relationship with God, through Christ, is the catalyst for growth and for changing into the likeness of God.

Yet God created people to need each other, too. In Genesis 2:18, God said it was not good that man was alone. When you think about it, you'll realize that Adam wasn't alone: He enjoyed a relationship with God and the animals he named (Genesis 2:19-20). It might seem odd to include animals as a viable means to meet human relational needs, but they make great companions—it's hard, for example, for me to imagine my life without a dog in it. And yet, even with all this company, God referred to Adam as being alone. Why? Because Adam was the only human being on the planet, and God created people to need people.

It is especially true that Christians need to keep company with other Christians (Ecclesiastes 4:12; Matthew 18:20). Believers, indwelt with the Holy Spirit (Ephesians 1:13), are an important source through which the love of God flows. I will discuss the significance of love in the Christ-formation process in a later chapter; for now, note that the love of God that is expressed from one believer to another is essential to Christ-formation.

Relationships with other believers are so important that they are tied to over fifty "one another" commands in the New Testament.[4] For example, the writer to the Hebrews said, "Let us consider how to stir up one another to love and good works, not neglecting to meet together" (Hebrews 10:24-25). New Testament scholar Joseph Hellerman writes about the essential role relationships play in the lives of believers:

> The New Testament church was decidedly strong-group in its social orientation, but this was no accident of cultural accommodation. Jesus unequivocally affirmed such an approach to interpersonal relationships when He chose "family" as the defining metaphor to describe His followers.[5]

God has placed a deep need in the human heart to belong and to be known by others, and he created the church—the family of God—in part to meet these needs. Richard Plass and James Cofield affirm the essential role human relationships play in our personal well-being:

> Relationships are not just important priorities. They are essential for our physical, psychological, emotional and spiritual well-being. We cannot live fully alive apart from loving connection with others.[6]

The family of God should be the safest people on Earth to share your deepest, darkest secrets without fear of being judged, criticized, rejected, or abandoned. In fact, believers are commanded to love and accept each other unconditionally in the same way they are loved and accepted by God (Romans 15:7).

As I write this chapter, I am "sheltering in place" due to the COVID-19 global pandemic. For five weeks—and for the foreseeable future—we have been ordered by federal and state authorities to practice social distancing, staying at least six feet away from others while in public. We are allowed to leave our homes only to run essential errands for food, medicine, and medical attention. This whole ordeal has been a profound reminder to me of how much I need human connection. Human touch is essential to human thriving, and I miss connecting with others through a handshake or a hug.

And yet, as important as relationships are to the Christ-formation process, there is a third ingredient we can't leave out: our own direct participation.

Ingredient #3: Direct Participation

Paul alludes to our direct participation in Philippians 2:12: "Work out your own salvation with fear and trembling." Notice that Paul says to "work out" your salvation, not to "work for" your salvation: There's a big difference between the two!

Throughout the New Testament, we find substantial evidence that a believer must participate in his or her own process of growth and change.

- "Present your bodies as a living sacrifice. . . . Do not be conformed to this world, but be transformed by the renewal of your mind" (Romans 12:1-2).

- "Submit yourselves therefore to God" (James 4:7).

- "Be watchful, stand firm in the faith, act like men, be strong. Let all that you do be done in love" (1 Corinthians 16:13-14).

- "Put off your old self . . . put on the new self" (Ephesians 4:22, 24).

- "Be imitators of God. . . . Walk in love" (Ephesians 5:1-2).

- "Rejoice in the Lord always" (Philippians 4:4).

- "What you have learned and received and heard and seen in me—practice these things" (Philippians 4:9).

- "Seek the things that are above. . . . Set your minds on things that are above" (Colossians 3:1-2).

- "Put on . . . compassionate hearts, kindness, humility, meekness, and patience, bearing with one another and, if one has a complaint against another, forgiving each other; as the Lord has forgiven you, so you also must forgive. And above all these put on love, which binds everything together in perfect harmony" (Colossians 3:12-14).

- "Let the peace of Christ rule in your hearts. . . . Be thankful" (Colossians 3:15).

- "Let the word of Christ dwell in you richly" (Colossians 3:16).

- "Whatever you do, in word or deed, do everything in the name of the Lord Jesus, giving thanks to God the Father through him" (Colossians 3:17).

- "Rejoice always, pray without ceasing, give thanks in all circumstances" (1 Thessalonians 5:16-18).

- "Train yourself for godliness" (1 Timothy 4:7).

- "Therefore, preparing your minds for action, and being sober-minded, set your hope fully on the grace that will be brought to you at the revelation of Jesus Christ" (1 Peter 1:13).

- "Put away all malice and all deceit and hypocrisy and envy and all slander" (1 Peter 2:1).

- "Abstain from the passions of the flesh" (1 Peter 2:11).

- "Whoever says he abides in him ought to walk in the same way in which he walked" (1 John 2:6).

This list is important because it reveals that direct participation is valid and essential to Christ-formation. But let me be clear: I'm not advocating a works-based salvation nor any form of legalism. Christ-formation is a grace-sustained partnership between the believer and the Holy Spirit that Paul refers to in Philippians 2:13: "It is God who works in you, both to will and to work for his good pleasure."

Let's look more closely at how God's grace is both a gift from God and the power that energizes Christ-formation.

Grace Is a Gift

What was the best Christmas present you received as a kid? Was it a new bike or skateboard? Maybe a Barbie doll and her boyfriend, Ken. If you were really lucky, maybe even a Barbie playhouse. When I was ten years old, I wanted a slot-car racing set: two little electric cars that you race around a track. In my mind, that was the best Christmas gift I could ever receive. I wanted this toy in the worst way, and I let my mom know for months before Christmas that if I got that toy, I would never ask for another toy again: I would finally be content.

On Christmas Eve, I accidently walked into my mom's bedroom while she was wrapping last-minute gifts to put under the tree. I quickly turned around, but as I did, I thought I caught a glimpse of a big box that looked a lot like a slot-car set. Oh man, was I excited. I didn't let on to what I had seen, but for the rest of the night before going to bed, I was bouncing around with excitement.

When Christmas morning came, I tore through the presents, but to my surprise, I found no slot-car set. And even though I had received some very nice gifts, I was disappointed. I couldn't figure it out. I was sure I saw it on Christmas Eve; were my eyes playing tricks on me? It didn't make any sense.

After all the presents were opened, my mom asked me to please go get a trash bag from the laundry room—way on the other side of the house—and start cleaning up the mess of opened boxes and shredded wrapping paper. When I got back to the living room and started cleaning up, my mom said, "Oh, honey, I think you missed a present." I was sure she was mistaken; I was very thorough about such things. She pointed out a large, unopened box hiding under a bunch of wrapping paper.

My mom is a tricky one. She knew that I had seen the slot-car set on the bed, but she wanted it to be a surprise. So when I went to get a trash bag, she ran to her room, grabbed the toy, and brought it back to the living room undetected. Once she pointed out the box, I ran over, tore it open, and there is was—in all its glory—the best Christmas gift ever!

How do you think my mom would have felt if, after opening the slot-car set, I had said, "How many months of my allowance is this going to cost me?" Or what about, "You know, Mom, after thinking about it, I don't deserve this gift. I acted like a spoiled little brat when I didn't find it under the tree." Neither of those remarks would have made her feel very good because the toy was a gift. Gifts are given out of love, not obligation.

In a similar way, our salvation is God's gift of love to whomever will receive it, no strings attached. Salvation is not something you can earn or deserve; God is love, and he wants everyone to be saved (1 Timothy 2:4) and to live with him in heaven for all eternity (John 14:2-3). And yet, God's grace is even more extravagant than going to heaven when you die.

The Unmerited Favor of God: The Gifts of Salvation

Grace is the gift that keeps on giving. Grace is the gift of eternal life: "The wages of sin is death, but the free gift of God is eternal life in Christ Jesus our Lord" (Romans 6:23). Grace is the gift of hope: "Now may our Lord Jesus Christ himself, and God our Father, who loved us and gave us eternal comfort and good hope through grace, comfort your hearts and establish them in every good work and word" (2 Thessalonians 2:16-17). Grace is a gift God decided to give you before you were born: "He who had set me apart before I was born, and who called me by his grace, was pleased to reveal his Son to me" (Galatians 1:15-16).

Grace is the gift of justification—a legal declaration that you are righteous before God in Christ: "Out of sheer generosity he put us in right standing with himself. A pure gift. He got us out of the mess we're in and restored us to where he always wanted us to be. And he did it by means of Jesus Christ" (Romans 3:24, MSG). The Holy Spirit is a gift of grace: "We know how dearly God loves us, because he has given us the Holy Spirit to fill our hearts with his love" (Romans 5:5, NLT). Grace is the gift of life and freedom: "Sin can't tell you how to live. After all, you're not living under that old tyranny any longer. You're living in the freedom of God" (Romans 6:14, MSG). Grace is God's gift of abundance: "Since he did not spare even his own Son but gave him up for us all, won't he also give us everything else?" (Romans 8:32, NLT).

Spiritual gifts are a gift of grace from God; they are given generously to believers to serve others and build up the body of Christ: "God's various gifts are handed out everywhere; but they all originate in God's Spirit. God's various ministries are carried out everywhere; but they all originate in God's Spirit" (1 Corinthians 12:4-6, MSG). Our life and every breath are gifts of grace: "He himself gives everyone life and breath and everything else" (Acts 17:25, NIV). All these and more are God's gifts of grace; they are given unconditionally and with love to every believer at the moment of salvation.

Philip Yancey recounts a story of when C. S. Lewis addressed a British conference on comparative religion. The participants were arguing about what made Christianity unique compared to all the other world religions. Lewis responded, "Oh, that's easy. It's grace." Yancy continues, "Only Christianity dares to make God's love unconditional."[7] And yet God's grace provides even more than these gifts of salvation.

The Unmerited Power of God: The Gifts of Christ-formation

Grace is the power of God that energizes our direct participation in Christ-formation. In other words, God's grace provides the will and ability to exert the effort that facilitates growth and change: "God is *working in you, giving you the desire and the power* to do what pleases him" (Philippians 2:13, NLT, emphasis added). Don't miss the fact that it is God who brings your will (the *desire*) and your ability to act (the *power*) into alignment with his good purpose. Peter makes a similar point: "By his divine power, God has given us everything we need for living a godly life" (2 Peter 1:3, NLT).

There is no conflict between God's grace and our direct participation in Christ-formation.

Therefore, God's grace is more than the gift of eternal life; it is also the source of all desire and ability to participate in our own Christ-formation. Author and philosopher Dallas Willard rightly pointed out that "grace is opposed to earning, but not to effort."[8] It is right to think about Christ-formation as an active—not passive—process energized by God's grace.

Consider the following biblical examples. God's grace provides the power of the Holy Spirit unto Christ-formation: "The Lord—who is the Spirit—makes us more and more like him as we are changed into his glorious image" (2 Corinthians 3:18, NLT). Grace provides the power to "do all things through him who strengthens [us]" (Philippians 4:13). Grace provides the power to control our thoughts:

> We use our powerful God-tools for smashing warped philosophies,
> tearing down barriers erected against the truth of God, fitting
> every loose thought and emotion and impulse into the structure of
> life shaped by Christ. Our tools are ready at hand for clearing the
> ground of every obstruction and building lives of obedience into
> maturity.
> 2 CORINTHIANS 10:5-6, MSG

Grace provides the power to stand against Satan's schemes: "Be strong in the Lord and in the strength of his might" (Ephesians 6:10). Grace provides the power to endure hardships. God's grace gave Paul the power to endure his thorn in the flesh: "My grace is sufficient for you, for my power is made perfect in weakness" (2 Corinthians 12:9). Spiritual gifts are both given and energized by grace: "Grace was given to each one of us according to the measure of Christ's gift" (Ephesians 4:7). God's grace comes to every believer in a diverse set of gifts that could never be deserved. Grace is both the power of God unto salvation and Christ-formation.

In this chapter, we have looked at three ingredients for Christ-formation: information (God's special and general revelation), relationships (with God and others), and direct participation energized by grace. The Holy Spirit energizes these ingredients with grace, and the result is a process for Christ-formation and a greater experience of the abundant life.

Restoring My Soul with God

1. Read and reflect on how God reveals himself through creation.

His invisible attributes, namely, his eternal power and divine nature, have been clearly perceived, ever since the creation of the world, in the things that have been made.

ROMANS 1:20

The heavens declare the glory of God,
    and the sky above proclaims his handiwork.
Day to day pours out speech,
    and night to night reveals knowledge.

PSALM 19:1-2

_____

_____

_____

2. Go for a walk in your neighborhood, at a park, at the beach, or in the mountains and make a list below of the things you see, hear, and smell that reveal aspects of God's character and divine nature.

1.	11.
2.	12.
3.	13.
4.	14.
5.	15.
6.	16.
7.	17.
8.	18.
9.	19.
10.	20.

In his book on spiritual exercises, *Journey with Jesus*, Larry Warner asks, "How do these things you are seeing speak without words to you about God and God's love and care"?[9] Apply Warner's question to the list you compiled on the previous page.

_____

_____

_____

Restoring My Soul with Others

1. Of the three ingredients for Christ-formation (information, relationships, and direct participation), which one is easiest for you to engage with? Why do you think so?

2. What do you learn about the Christ-formation process through special and general revelation?

3. What do you learn about the Christ-formation process through relationships with God and others?

4. What do you learn about the Christ-formation process through direct participation?

5. How is God's grace the source of Christ-formation?

6. Has this chapter changed your understanding about God's grace? How?

4

THE ABUNDANT LIFE IS
A MATTER OF THE HEART

SOMETHING AMAZING HAPPENS TO you at the moment of salvation; you are placed "in Christ." This phrase is found throughout Paul's letters in the New Testament and describes a new reality that includes the forgiveness of sin (Ephesians 1:7-8; Colossians 1:13-14), a life free from condemnation (Romans 8:1), a new identity as a son or daughter of God (Galatians 4:1-8), and a new position as a coheir with Christ (Romans 8:17). Now, everything that Jesus has is yours (Hebrews 1:2), including his glory (John 17:22) and his riches (2 Corinthians 8:9).

But that's not all. Because you are "in Christ," the Holy Spirit (or "Spirit of Jesus"; see Acts 16:6-7) lives in you (1 Corinthians 3:16). He secures your salvation for the rest of eternity (Ephesians 2:13-14), strengthens you with God's power (Ephesians 3:16), and guides you into all truth (John 16:13). The Spirit comforts you in times of pain (2 Corinthians 1:4), intercedes for you in prayer (Romans 8:26), pours God's love into your heart (Romans 5:5), affirms in your spirit that you are a child of God (Romans 8:16), and provides you with the desire and power to live a godly life (Philippians 2:13; 2 Peter 1:3).

All this and more is true of you and complete in you at the moment of salvation. And if this were not enough, Jesus actually lives in your heart, your inner being (Romans 8:10; 2 Corinthians 13:5; Galatians 2:20; Colossians 1:27). Not only are you "in Christ," Christ is in you.

Jesus described this reality using the illustration of a vine and a branch:

> Abide in me, and I in you. As the branch cannot bear fruit by itself, unless it abides in the vine, neither can you, unless you abide in me. I am the vine; you are the branches. Whoever abides in me and I in him, he it is that bears much fruit, for apart from me you can do nothing. If anyone does not abide in me he is thrown away like a branch and withers; and the branches are gathered, thrown into the fire, and burned. If you abide in me, and my words abide in you, ask whatever you wish, and it will be done for you. By this my Father is glorified, that you bear much fruit and so prove to be my disciples.
> JOHN 15:4-8

The "fruit" which Jesus is referring to includes the attributes of his own character, namely love. As such, from the moment of your salvation, the Holy Spirit begins the Christ-formation process in your heart, helping you take on the character traits of Jesus. This is what Paul was referring to in his letter to the Corinthians: "The Lord—who is the Spirit—makes us more and more like him as we are changed into his glorious image" (2 Corinthians 3:18, NLT). Another way to think about this Christlike character is to liken it to the fruit of the Spirit. Paul writes, "The Holy Spirit produces this kind of fruit in our lives: love, joy, peace, patience, kindness, goodness, faithfulness, gentleness, and self-control" (Galatians 5:22-23, NLT). These Christlike character qualities are what make you more like Jesus and promote a certain quality of life that is similar to the life that Jesus experienced when he was on Earth.

Jesus never worried about what he would eat, or the clothing he would wear, or where he would sleep. He trusted his Father to provide all these things (Matthew 6:25-34). Jesus never pursued wealth, position, or power. In fact, when Satan offered those things to Jesus in the wilderness, he turned them down (Matthew 4:1-11). Even though Jesus experienced all the difficulties, temptations, and human limitations inherent to life on planet Earth—except for sin (Hebrews 4:15)—he lived in a state of shalom, free from all the attachments and grievances associated with this world. And this same quality of life is available for you.

You may be thinking, *If Jesus has made his character and quality of life available to me today, why am I not experiencing more of it?* The answer might be simpler than you think.

The Biblical Emphasis on Right Thinking

Second only to loving relationships with God and others, right thinking affects Christ-formation and abundant living. We will discuss the role of healthy relational attachment in Christ-formation more fully in a later chapter, but in this book, I'm going to focus on the cognitive options, as those are where we have the most direct control and can make our best start. What we choose to think about matters—a lot!

More passages in the New Testament emphasize the importance of right thinking than you realize. Once you start looking for them, you will see them everywhere. A similar thing happens when you buy a new car. Let's say you decided to buy a new white Honda Civic. Before buying it, you hardly noticed another white Honda Civic on the road. But after buying it and driving it off the lot, you see the same car everywhere. Why? Because after buying the car, you have a different frame of reference: Essentially, we see what we want to see.

The same is true when you start reading the Bible for evidence of how important right thinking is for your quality of life in Christ. Here are a few examples (emphasis mine):

- "Be transformed by the *renewal of your mind*" (Romans 12:2).

- "We destroy arguments and every lofty opinion raised against the knowledge of God, and *take every thought captive to obey Christ*" (2 Corinthians 10:5).

- "Since you have heard about Jesus and have learned the truth that comes from him, throw off your old sinful nature and your former way of life, which is corrupted by lust and deception. Instead, *let the Spirit renew your thoughts and attitudes*. Put on your new nature, created to be like God—truly righteous and holy" (Ephesians 4:21-24, NLT).

- "Finally, brothers, whatever is true, whatever is honorable, whatever is just, whatever is pure, whatever is lovely, whatever is commendable, if there is any excellence, if there is anything worthy of praise, *think about* these things" (Philippians 4:8).

- "*Set your minds* on things above, not on earthly things" (Colossians 3:2, NIV).

These are just a few examples. The fact is, what you choose to think about directly—especially the thoughts you choose to think about God, yourself, and others—will dramatically affect your quality of life in Christ. In order to explain how this works, let me begin with a biblical theology of the soul.

A Biblical Theology of the Soul

Human beings are composed of two primary parts that I will refer to in this book as the *material self* and the *immaterial self*. Paul identifies these parts as the "outer self" that is "wasting away" and the "inner self" that is "being renewed day by day" (2 Corinthians 4:16). The material part of a person is their body, consisting of eleven organ systems that work together as a collective. For example, if you are crossing the street and see that you are about to be hit by an oncoming car, your outer self goes into immediate action by activating a complex cadre of bodily systems—known as a stress response—that helps you get out of the way.

The immaterial part of a person is what Paul refers to as the "inner self" and includes thoughts, emotions, and will (or desire—the place where people make decisions). There are four words in the Bible that refer to the inner self: *heart, inner being, mind*, and *spirit*.

Think of your soul as a bucket that contains both your material and immaterial parts. The soul is the totality of what makes up who you are as a human being created in the image and likeness of God.

When God created Adam, the Bible says, "The LORD God formed the man of dust from the ground and breathed into his nostrils the breath of life, and the man became a living creature" (Genesis 2:7). It is important to notice that this creation account includes both the outer self (material) and the inner self (immaterial). The Hebrew word for "creature" is *nephesh*, which literally means "soul." To be a living soul requires two aspects: a body (material) and a Spirit (immaterial) (see Figure 4.1).

God created human beings to live as integrated and whole beings. The

FIGURE 4.1

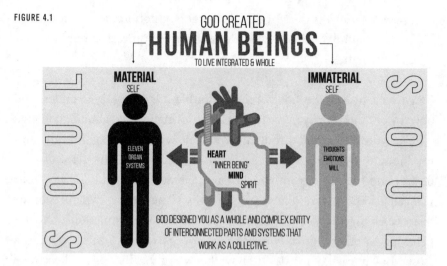

various aspects of the material and immaterial self are directly involved in the process of Christ-formation and the abundant life.

Christ-Formation Takes Place in the Heart

The Bible often uses the word *heart* to describe the immaterial aspect of the self.[1] Solomon writes, "Guard your heart above all else, for it determines the course of your life" (Proverbs 4:23, NLT). Jesus referred to the heart as the operation center for all behavior, including good and evil: "Out of the abundance of the heart the mouth speaks. The good person out of his good treasure brings forth good, and the evil person out of his evil treasure brings forth evil" (Matthew 12:34-35). Jesus said the Great Commandment is lived out from the heart (Mark 12:30) and in the Sermon on the Mount, he blesses the pure in heart (Matthew 5:8). Paul maintains that the presence of Christ resides in the heart (Galatians 4:6). According to the Bible, the heart is the operation center for all of life and is in the process of being formed in Christ. Biblical scholar and theology professor Robert Saucy explained,

> The heart is the control center of life. It is the place where God works to change us and the place we also must work if growth is to take place. . . .
>
> God works his renewal in and through our heart. . . . *The heart*

is who we are. It is the seat of our thoughts, emotions, and actions. Understanding the heart will help us grasp the process of our transformation.[2]

Because the heart is the "control center" for life, it is necessary to understand how it works, especially in regard to Christ-formation and abundant living.

The word *heart* used throughout the Bible is composed of three dynamics: thought, emotion, and will. (Think of your will as the place of your desires and the place from which you make decisions and choices. Your will can also be understood as your identity.) These three dynamics of the heart work together—much like the gears in a car transmission—to drive behavior. In other words, *human behavior begins in the heart.* Let's take a closer look at each dynamic and how they work together as a collective to influence behavior.

Gear #1: Thinking Is a Dynamic of the Heart

It seems counterintuitive, but thinking is a function of the heart before it is an action carried out in the brain. What is meant by thinking cannot be reduced to the synaptic activity in the brain; to think is a mysterious process that operates outside the basic mechanics of the body. It is a matter first of spirit, of "heart."

Throughout Scripture, we find this idea that thinking begins in the heart. Moses told the Israelites that the Lord had given them a heart to understand his ways (Deuteronomy 29:4). Throughout the book of Proverbs, the heart is referred to as the place of knowing: "Apply your heart to instruction and your ear to words of knowledge" (Proverbs 23:12); "The heart of him who has understanding seeks knowledge" (Proverbs 15:14). God promised to give his people a heart to know him (Jeremiah 24:7). The apostle Paul prayed for the Romans: "Having the eyes of your hearts enlightened, that you may know what is the hope to which [God] has called you, what are the riches of his glorious inheritance in the saints" (Ephesians 1:18). These verses, and a number of others, affirm that thinking begins in the heart.

Of the three dynamics of the heart—thought, emotion, and will—primacy of place is given by the Bible to thought. Old Testament scholar Hans Walter Wolff wrote: "In by far the greatest number of cases it is intellectual, rational functions that are ascribed to the heart."[3] Yet, feelings are closely intertwined: Feelings are directly affected by thoughts. Dallas Willard wrote,

Feeling and thought always go together. They are interdependent and are never found apart. There is no feeling without something being before the mind in thought and no thought without some positive or negative feeling toward what is contemplated. . . .

The connection between thought and feeling is so intimate that the "mind" is usually treated as consisting of thought and feeling *together.*[4]

In the Bible, therefore, emotions are second in emphasis to thoughts, and both elements reside in the heart.

Gear #2: Emotion Is a Dynamic of the Heart

Throughout the Bible, we find numerous verses that indicate the important role emotions play in the heart. For example, Peter writes that love resides in the heart (1 Peter 1:22). Jesus implied that love for God comes from the heart (Mark 12:30). Joy is an emotion that resides in the heart (Proverbs 15:15), as does peace (Colossians 3:15).

Conversely, the Bible affirms that hate resides in the heart (Leviticus 19:17), as well as fear (John 14:27). Feelings of sorrow also reside in the heart. Paul writes, "I have great sorrow and unceasing anguish in my heart" (Romans 9:2), and David laments, "How long must I wrestle with my thoughts and day after day have sorrow in my heart?" (Psalm 13:2, NIV).

Gear #3: The Will Is a Dynamic of the Heart

The Bible also refers to the heart as the place of the will. For example, God sent the flood to destroy the Earth because "The LORD saw that the wickedness of man was great in the earth, and that every intention of the thoughts of his heart was only evil continually" (Genesis 6:5). When Peter, led by the Holy Spirit, confronted Ananias and Sapphira about their sin of withholding money from the Lord, he recognized that each had "contrived this deed in [their] heart" (Acts 5:4). Paul warned the Corinthians not to judge each other because only the Lord knows the intent of the heart (1 Corinthians 4:5). And the writer to the Hebrews declared that God's Word "judges the thoughts and attitudes of the heart" (Hebrews 4:12, NIV). Figure 4.2 (top of next page) illustrates the three dynamics of the heart.

FIGURE 4.2

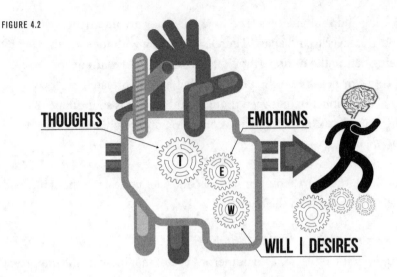

You don't have to be an engineer to realize that three gears lock together and that a fourth gear is necessary to generate movement. This fourth gear represents the final dynamic of the heart.

Gear #4: Revelation or Lies

The fourth gear can either work for us or against us. Depending on what it represents, it can turn all the other gears in a constructive or destructive way. If this gear represents God's revelation, it will promote healthy thoughts, emotions, and desires that will work out in our behavior (Figure 4.3). For example,

FIGURE 4.3

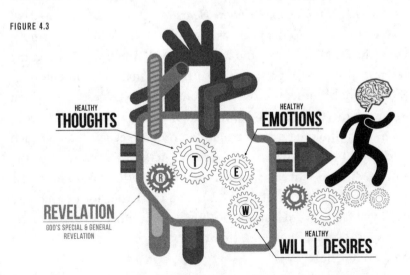

if I think about God's loving-kindness toward me and his ability to control all things by his power, I will feel safe and secure and not let fear control me.

However, the opposite is also true (Figure 4.4). If this gear represents lies and choosing to believe that God is not loving nor kind and all-powerful, I will be afraid. This thinking can produce a variety of unpleasant emotions, "including sadness, anger, fear, shame, hopeless despair, and disgust."[5] These unpleasant emotions affect the will and can play out in behavior in very destructive ways. Dumping a toxic amount of stress into our bodies can result in all kinds of destructive behavior.

FIGURE 4.4

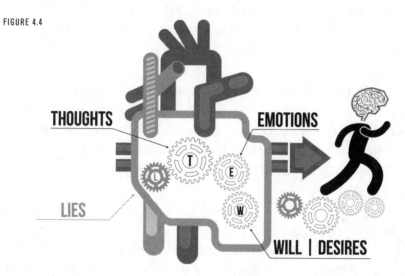

The dissonance between revelation and lies promotes the spiritual/emotional conflicts that hinder Christ-formation and abundant living. Therefore, we need to pay careful attention to the dynamics of the heart, especially by being mindful of our thoughts.

Of the four gears, the only one we can directly control long term is Gear #1: Thoughts. We cannot control our emotions directly, and willpower is unsustainable over the long term, but God has given us free will to choose the thoughts we will think. With my thoughts, I can choose the fourth gear. I can decide if I'm going to think thoughts based on God's truth or Satan's lies. Exercising our free will in regard to thoughts reveals how thinking directly affects how we live. Author and theology professor James Bryan Smith writes, "The primary practice of living as a Christian boils down to what we think about, what we dwell on, what values we keep before our minds, what truths (or lies) we have in our consciousness."[6] Again, the power behind our thoughts is reflected in Scripture.

Paul commands believers to "set your minds on things that are above, not on things that are on earth" (Colossians 3:2). This means that "every thought, aim, value, aspiration, and striving should come under his lordship."[7] When I set my mind on things above, I think about God's presence in my life and his grace and love for me as his son. I remember that no matter what is going on in my life, Jesus is with me and has everything under control.

I also make it a practice to dwell on the various aspects of my identity in Christ (see Appendix C). As I do, I feel grateful and loved. Additionally, in Philippians 4:8-9 (TPT), Paul offers a wonderful list of things to think about:

Keep your thoughts continually fixed on all that is authentic and real, honorable and admirable, beautiful and respectful, pure and holy, merciful and kind. And fasten your thoughts on every glorious work of God, praising him always. Follow the example of all that we have imparted to you and the God of peace will be with you in all things.

The Greek word *logizomai* (translated here as "keep your thoughts continually fixed" and "fasten your thoughts") essentially means to occupy your mind constantly with something. Here, that something ("authentic and real, honorable and admirable, beautiful and respectful, pure and holy, merciful and kind . . . every glorious work of God") is nothing less than the things of God. Of course, Paul may not have understood the nuances of neuroscience, but the Holy Spirit sure does, and as he inspired Paul's writing, he emphasized the importance of constantly being mindful of the things of God. In fact, the more consistently we choose to focus our thoughts on the things of God, the more consistently we will experience a state of peace (Isaiah 26:3).

As a senior pastor, after my closing prayer each Sunday, I offered the benediction to the congregation. I did this for many years to remind them to keep their minds fixed on the true God throughout the week. I want to encourage you to do the same, to keep one eye on eternity every moment of the day: Keep your thoughts fixed on things above. Choose to think about "all that is authentic and real, honorable and admirable, beautiful and respectful, pure and holy, merciful and kind." And in the midst of whatever challenges you may face, ground yourself in the reality of God's loving presence. God has given you the power to choose what you think about. Choose wisely, and you will experience his peace.

Restoring My Soul with God

Take ten minutes during the next five days and work through the following questions. (Doing these exercises for ten minutes each day for five days will create a strong neural connection with the truth.)

DAY 1: Read through Appendix C: "My Identity in Christ." Write down the top ten traits that stand out to you below. What do you notice about God? What would you like to thank God for?

1. _____

2. _____

3. _____

4. _____

5. _____

6. _____

7. _____

8. _____

9. _____

10. _____

_____

_____

_____

_____

DAY 2: Choose three identity traits (from your list above) that are the most meaningful to you and write out the trait along with the verse in the space below. Limit this exercise to ten minutes.

1. _____

_____

_____

2. _____

_____

_____

3. _____

_____

_____

Why are these traits so meaningful to you?

_____

_____

_____

DAYS 3–5: For the next three days, read through the entire list each day and list ten different things each day that stand out to you.

Restoring My Soul with Others

1. How is the fruit of the Spirit described in this chapter? What is the fruit? Do you agree?

2. How would you describe the heart and its role in Christ-formation?

3. In your own words, how would you describe the three dynamics of the heart? How do you see them working together to drive behavior?

4. What is "right thinking," and why is it such an important aspect in Christ-formation?

5

SIN AS THE HINDRANCE TO CHRIST-FORMATION

CHRIST-FORMATION IS BASED ON the premise that people are relational beings who grow and thrive—emotionally and spiritually—within the context of relationships with God and others. These relationships provide the emotional connections that are necessary for healthy human development. Psychologist Henry Cloud explains,

> Bonding is one of the most basic and foundational ideas in life and the universe. It is a basic human need. God created us with a hunger for relationship—for relationship with him and with our fellow people. At our very core we are relational beings. Without a solid, bonded relationship, the human soul will become mired in psychological and emotional problems. The soul cannot prosper without being connected to others. No matter what characteristics we possess, or what accomplishments we amass, without solid emotional connectedness, without bonding to God and other humans, we . . . will suffer sickness of the soul.[1]

Therefore, relational connection or bonding is a fundamental human need; this is made evident in the creation account.

People Are Created in the Image of God

God is a relational being who exists in a loving, triune community as Father, Son, and Holy Spirit (see, for example, the plural language of Genesis 1:26). Loving relationship is the essence of God's being. Since God created human beings in his own image and likeness (again, see Genesis 1:26), we know that people are relational beings, requiring loving connection with God and other people in order to thrive. Henry Cloud writes, "Without relationship, without attachment to God and others, we can't be our true selves. We can't be truly human."[2]

Just as loving relationships within the triune community are fundamental to the nature of God, so loving relationships are fundamental to the nature of every person who is created in the image of God. A greater understanding of our relational nature and needs is essential for Christ-formation and the ability to experience the abundant life. The bottom line is this: You cannot grow in Christ and thrive by yourself; you must be connected in an intimate and loving relationship with God and other people. These connections become the very conduits of love that is essential for emotional health and spiritual growth inherent in the Christ-formation process. The first and primary relationship that you need in order to thrive is a relationship with God.

People Need Relationship

When God created Adam, he did so in a unique and personal way: "The LORD God formed the man of dust from the ground and breathed into his nostrils the breath of life, and the man became a living creature" (Genesis 2:7). God lovingly fashioned Adam with personal attention and great care and then intimately breathed life into him. It was as if God knelt over Adam, placed his mouth over Adam's mouth, and breathed divine life into his body. God demonstrated the same personal and loving approach when he created Eve (Genesis 2:22).

This intimacy between God, Adam, and Eve provides evidence of God's love and infuses human beings with immense value and worth. God created human beings for relationship—first and foremost—with himself.

The primacy of the human relationship with God was made evident when God placed him in the Garden, providing him with food (Genesis 2:9) and companionship (Genesis 2:20).

Yet Adam was not complete without human companionship (Genesis 2:18). God provides us with a variety of human relationships to help us grow and thrive. These relationships begin in our immediate family (Ephesians 6:4), develop further in friendships (Ecclesiastes 4:9-12)—especially within the body of Christ (1 Corinthians 12:12-13)—and reach their ultimate expression in marriage, as husband and wife become one flesh (Genesis 2:24). Anthony Hoekema writes,

> The human person is not an isolated being who is complete in himself or herself. . . .
>
> Men and women cannot attain to true humanity in isolation; they need the fellowship and stimulation of others. We are social beings. The very fact that man is told to love his neighbor as himself implies that man needs his neighbor.
>
> Man cannot be truly human apart from others.[3]

The truth is, you matter to God. Christ-formation leads us into a greater quality of intimacy with God—the essence of the abundant life.

The loving care that God demonstrated when creating Adam and Eve means a lot to me because from the time I was a little boy, I have struggled with feelings of insecurity and fear. My early childhood experiences with bullying and the abandonment and rejection I felt as a result of my parents' divorce planted seeds of shame and fear deep within my heart that I still struggle with today. I have to remind myself—sometimes many times a day—how much God loves me. I struggle to believe at times that I matter to God. I'm guessing that you wonder about that at times too. But let this truth penetrate deeply into your heart: God loves you more than you can possibly imagine, even on your worst day. God's love is constant; it does not ebb and flow depending on our behavior. The fact is, God loves you and me in this moment as much as he will ever love us.

In fact, God loved us before the creation of the world. Paul writes about this in Ephesians 1:4-6:

Long before he laid down earth's foundations, he had us in mind, had settled on us as the focus of his love, to be made whole and holy by his love. Long, long ago he decided to adopt us into his family through Jesus Christ. (What pleasure he took in planning this!) He wanted us to enter into the celebration of his lavish gift-giving by the hand of his beloved Son.

EPHESIANS 1:4-6, MSG

Knowing, believing, and abiding in God's love fuels Christ-formation and the abundant life. As you live in the reality of God's love for you revealed in Scripture, confirmed in your heart by the Holy Spirit, and demonstrated by close friends, you will experience a different quality of life. This is the quality of life that Adam and Eve experienced before the Fall. But tragically, sin changed everything.

Sin Changed Everything

Prior to the Fall, Adam and Eve enjoyed unbroken intimacy with God and each other as they lived in the Garden without shame (Genesis 3:8). After the Fall, instead of enjoying life-giving relationships, Adam and Eve experienced death, resulting in isolation and a foreign, chaotic state of existence characterized by feelings of shame and fear. Robert Saucy wrote,

> On the day that man sinned, he experienced personal separation from God resulting in the death of spirit or the inner person. This was immediately evident in his hiding from God in fear (Gen. 3:8, 10). Spiritual death not only signified alienation from God, but also resulted in alienation from his fellow human being (Gen. 3:12). Moreover, it brought disorder to man's inner being. For the first time he experienced the inner chaos of shame and guilt.[4]

When Adam and Eve sinned, they experienced "heart damage." Theologians and professors Gordon Lewis and Bruce Demarest comment on Adam and Eve's damaged inner condition:

> Inwardly Adam and Eve were now lawbreakers and rebels against the Lawgiver. Their hearts, the very centers of their natures, had

become deceitful and desperately wicked. Instead of being loving creatures in reflecting God's likeness, they had become insolent.[5]

As a result of sin, the relationships Adam and Eve enjoyed with God and each other were severed. Loving connection was replaced with shame, fear, and the desire to hide (Genesis 3:7-12). Thriving was replaced with striving and pain (Genesis 3:16-19). The former state of inner tranquility was replaced with a chaotic state of the heart that promoted spiritual/emotional conflicts: lies and distortions about God, self, and each other.

The universal effects of the Fall can be summed up in one word: death. In order to make progress in Christ-formation and a greater experience of the abundant life, we must understand the consequences of death.

The Implications of Death

Prior to Creation, "Earth was a soup of nothingness, a bottomless emptiness, an inky blackness. God's Spirit brooded like a bird above the watery abyss" (Genesis 1:2, MSG). Out of this formless void, God brought order and beauty, culminating in the creation of human beings. The rebellion against God was a choice to return to the chaos. The unexpected consequence of sin was to welcome back the "abyss" of "inky blackness."

Death as the result of sin informs two aspects that hinder Christ-formation and the abundant life. The first consequence is human isolation

FIGURE 5.1

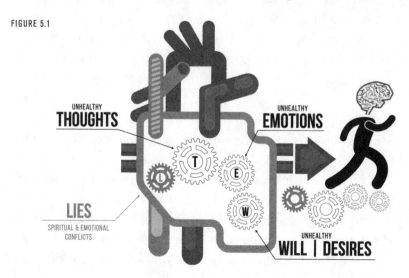

UNHEALTHY
THOUGHTS

UNHEALTHY
EMOTIONS

LIES
SPIRITUAL & EMOTIONAL
CONFLICTS

UNHEALTHY
WILL | DESIRES

due to broken relationships with God and others, and the second consequence is an inner chaotic condition of the heart that promotes lies and feelings of shame, which are inherent in spiritual/emotional conflicts (see Figure 5.1).

Because human beings thrive in the context of loving relationships, psychologist and author John Townsend writes, "Isolation is our most injurious state. . . . Whatever is cut off tends toward deterioration."[6] Thus, relational isolation produces inner chaos in the heart. In fact, John Townsend and Henry Cloud boldly assert,

> At the emotional level, connection is the sustaining factor for
> the psyche, the heart, and the spirit. Virtually every emotional
> and psychological problem, from addictions to depression, has
> alienation or emotional isolation at its core or close to it. Recovery
> from these problems always involves helping people to get more
> connected to each other at deeper and healthier levels than
> they are.[7]

Prior to the Fall, Adam and Eve "were both naked, and they felt no shame" (Genesis 2:25, NIV). The first couple lived in a state of vulnerability with each other and with God. After the Fall, however, we read an entirely different story. Adam and Eve covered their nakedness with fig leaves and "hid themselves from the presence of the LORD" (Genesis 3:7-8). This state of hiding, or isolation, is a by-product of sin and is often the point of origin of our deceptive thinking that contributes to our spiritual/emotional conflicts. In other words, we are more prone to distorted thinking and more susceptible to the lies of Satan when we are alone.

Thankfully, the aftermath of sin is not the end of the story; God's loving-kindness prevails as he provides the way of escape from the consequences of sin and death. The good news of the gospel is that death—as a consequence of sin—has been defeated; Jesus' atoning work on the cross literally removes death as the repercussion for sin. This means that as a Christian, you can be confident that at the moment of salvation your sin is forgiven (Ephesians 1:7; 1 John 1:9). You are a new creation in Christ (Romans 8:1) and a child of God (John 1:12-13). Forgiveness restores your relationship with God, fills you with God's Holy Spirit, and enables you to love God and others (1 John 4:19). Jesus Christ restores the relational connection that was lost after the Fall and begins an inner transformation of the heart that promotes spiritual/emotional vitality.

And yet, God doesn't wipe clean our memories of hurt and pain. Many of the spiritual/emotional conflicts produced by sin remain and must be worked out in the context of relationships. In the next chapter, I will discuss the nature of these spiritual/emotional conflicts and show you how they hinder Christ-formation and abundant living.

Restoring My Soul with God

The following five-day exercises are designed to help you internalize the depths of God's love. Take ten minutes each day to read and reflect on the passage. Circle any words and phrases that jump out at you, then pause for a few minutes to write down whatever God speaks to your heart. Make note of anything you want to share with your group.

DAY 1: God demonstrated his love for me at the cross:

> This is how God showed his love for us: God sent his only Son into the world so we might live through him. This is the kind of love we are talking about—not that we once upon a time loved God, but that he loved us and sent his Son as a sacrifice to clear away our sins and the damage they've done to our relationship with God.
>
> 1 JOHN 4:9-10, MSG

_____

_____

_____

DAY 2: God's love for me is absolute:

> God has made us to be more than conquerors, and his demonstrated love is our glorious victory over everything!

So now I live with the confidence that there is nothing
in the universe with the power to separate us from God's
love. I'm convinced that his love will triumph over death,
life's troubles, fallen angels, or dark rulers in the heavens.
There is nothing in our present or future circumstances
that can weaken his love. There is no power above us
or beneath us—no power that could ever be found in
the universe that can distance us from God's passionate
love, which is lavished upon us through our Lord Jesus,
the Anointed One!

ROMANS 8:37-39, TPT

DAY 3: God's love for me is too great to understand:

I pray that from his glorious, unlimited resources he will
empower you with inner strength through his Spirit. Then
Christ will make his home in your hearts as you trust in
him. Your roots will grow down into God's love and keep
you strong. And may you have the power to understand,
as all God's people should, how wide, how long, how high,
and how deep his love is. May you experience the love of
Christ, though it is too great to understand fully. Then
you will be made complete with all the fullness of life and
power that comes from God.

EPHESIANS 3:16-19, NLT

DAY 4: God's love for me is perfect and unending:

> Love is patient and kind; love does not envy or boast; it is
> not arrogant or rude. It does not insist on its own way; it is
> not irritable or resentful; it does not rejoice at wrongdoing,
> but rejoices with the truth. Love bears all things, believes
> all things, hopes all things, endures all things.
>   Love never ends.
>
> 1 CORINTHIANS 13:4-8

_____

_____

_____

DAY 5: God's love drives away fear:

> God is love, and all who live in love live in God, and God
> lives in them. And as we live in God, our love grows more
> perfect. So we will not be afraid on the day of judgment,
> but we can face him with confidence because we live like
> Jesus here in this world.
>   Such love has no fear, because perfect love expels all
> fear. If we are afraid, it is for fear of punishment, and this
> shows that we have not fully experienced his perfect love.
> We love each other because he loved us first.
>
> 1 JOHN 4:16-19, NLT

_____

_____

_____

Restoring My Soul with Others

1. Why are relationships with God and others fundamental to Christ-formation?

2. Take turns reading out loud the story about Ruth, Naomi, and Boaz in the Old Testament book of Ruth. List in the space below the principles you notice that support the idea that people need people.

_____

_____

_____

3. How does growing in intimacy with God and others contribute to a greater experience of the abundant life?

6

THE SPIRITUAL/EMOTIONAL CONFLICTS THAT HINDER CHRIST-FORMATION

JENNIFER BECAME A CHRISTIAN as a teenager. During high school, she was a leader in the church's youth group where her family attended. She actively served in the children's ministry and community-outreach projects and participated in a couple of mission trips to Guatemala and Peru. The source of Jennifer's love to serve came out of her devotional life. She spent significant time in prayer and Bible study and took long walks on the beach to be alone with God. By all accounts, Jennifer had a deeply personal relationship with Jesus.

When Jennifer was a junior in college, she was sexually assaulted while walking back to her dorm one night. During the months of intensive therapy that followed this traumatic event, Jennifer realized that she was feeling an uncomfortable dissonance with God as she struggled to align what she believed to be true about God—that he was her all-powerful, loving heavenly Father—and her experience of being assaulted. Jennifer found herself stuck in a deeply disturbing cycle of doubts: *Is God truly ever present and all-powerful? Is God with me? Does he love me? Can I trust him to protect me?* The dissonance Jennifer was experiencing is what I refer to as spiritual/emotional conflict.

Spiritual/emotional conflicts often emerge from human hurt or a traumatic experience. Your perception of God will cause you to either move toward him or away from him. So distorted perceptions of God must be confronted and corrected in order for us to experience the abundant life.

The Origin of Spiritual/Emotional Conflicts

Maybe your situation is not as traumatic as Jennifer's, but all of us, at one time or another, find it difficult to align our beliefs about God with certain experiences. Pastor and professor James Hamilton explains this dynamic tension:

> Psychologists are keenly aware that there can be a great gap
> between what one knows and how one feels. . . . This cleavage can
> also be experienced in regard to one's relationship with God. Thus,
> while one's knowledge of God may be valid, the way that one feels
> about God may be distorted.[1]

The gap between knowledge and feelings created by a painful experience not only affects how we see God but can often distort how we perceive God thinks and feels about us. For example, the Gallup organization surveyed 1,721 Christian college students and found that 31 percent agreed with the following statement: "God is quite angry and is capable of meting out punishment to those who are unfaithful or ungodly."[2] It's not hard to imagine how this type of thinking would adversely affect one's relationship with God. If we believe that God is constantly angry and ready to throw a lightning bolt at us, we're going to live in fear and try to stay as far away from God as we can.

To believe that God lives in a perpetual bad mood is a complete distortion of the truth. I recognize that there are examples in the Scriptures of God being angry with the Israelites (2 Samuel 24; 2 Kings 17:18), and I know the Bible teaches that God will one day judge unbelievers (Revelation 20:12-15). But God is not a smoldering volcano of wrath waiting to erupt at our slightest misstep. In fact, God revealed himself to Moses as "a God of mercy and grace, endlessly patient—so much love, so deeply true—loyal in love for a thousand generations, forgiving iniquity, rebellion, and sin"

(Exodus 34:6-7, MSG). Yes, God is holy, righteous, and just, and he punishes sin (Exodus 34:7). But those attributes are not in conflict with God's loving, compassionate, and merciful nature.

It's important that we check our thoughts and feelings about God at the door of biblical truth because a distorted perception of God will carry over into a distorted perception of self. James Hamilton argues, "There is a significant correlation between a negative view of God and low self-concept. . . . Almost without exception I find that persons who have negative views of God also have negative views of themselves."[3] Hamilton goes on to say that spiritual/emotional conflicts are mutually reinforcing:

> One's view of God is the foundational issue. If that view is valid, it makes for both health and happiness. If the view of God is distorted, it results in feelings of alienation from Him, feelings of alienation from oneself and often feelings of alienation from others.[4]

The lies inherent in distortions about God and self can generate thinking patterns that produce unhealthy emotions. These affect decision making and can ultimately drive behavior that takes us away from God. In order to resolve these conflicts, we need to review the dynamics of the heart.

In chapter 4, we discovered the fourth gear in the heart that can either work for us or against us. If lies are driving the fourth gear, distorted thoughts and damaging emotions may influence the will toward sinful behavior. If God's truth is driving the fourth gear, however, an entirely different outcome will ensue. Distorted thinking will be replaced with biblical thinking, which will promote healthy emotions, which will influence the will toward behavior that's in keeping with the fruit of the Spirit.

No metaphor is perfect, but the gear metaphor offers a visual example of how thought, emotion, and will work together. They are affected by lies or truth; they drive behavior. All these dynamics are taking place in the heart (Proverbs 4:23; Luke 6:45).

God didn't reform the heart; instead, he gave each of us a new one.

I will give you a new heart—I will give you new and right desires—
and put a new spirit within you. I will take out your stony hearts of
sin and give you new hearts of love. And I will put my Spirit within
you so that you will obey my laws and do whatever I command.

EZEKIEL 36:26-27, TLB

The context of these verses shows God is referring directly to the
Israelites, but this truth applies to you and me today. The good news of the
gospel isn't only about the forgiveness of sin and a home in heaven when
we die; it also involves becoming a "new creation" in Christ (2 Corinthians
5:17). That means, in part, that the former self—that deceitful and wicked
heart (Jeremiah 17:9)—is now dead, crucified with Christ (Romans 6:6).
The self that was enslaved to sin and consumed with "the lust of the flesh,
the lust of the eyes, and the pride of life" (1 John 2:16, NIV) is now no longer
in control. God gives every believer a new heart and a new capacity to live
with him and for him.

So, why do we still struggle to do good? Because the deceptive thought
patterns from the old heart remain like old habits. The lies we choose to
believe are the lingering thoughts associated with different experiences.
Dallas Willard described this dynamic using the words *spirit* and *heart*
interchangeably:

> The human spirit is an inescapable, fundamental aspect of every
> human being; and it takes on whichever character it has from the
> experiences and the choices that we have lived through or made
> in our past. . . .
>
> Our life and how we find the world now and in the future
> is, almost totally, a simple result of what we have become in the
> depths of our being—in our spirit, will, or heart. From there
> we see our world and interpret reality. From there we make
> our choices, break forth into action, try to change our world.[5]

Our entire being is shaped by experience. When the hurt from past
painful experiences lingers unresolved, it can affect what we believe to be
true. These beliefs commingle with other beliefs—whether influenced by
lies or truth—to compose what is often referred to as a worldview.

How My Worldview Influences My Heart

A worldview is a philosophical term that refers to how we view reality and the purpose of life. Author and editor James W. Sire provided a helpful definition:

> A worldview is a commitment, a fundamental orientation of the heart, that can be expressed as a story or in a set of presuppositions (assumptions which may be true, partially true or entirely false) which we hold (consciously or subconsciously, consistently or inconsistently) about the basic constitution of reality, and that provides the foundation on which we live and move and have our being.[6]

In other words, *a worldview isn't necessarily built on truth*. It can also be informed by lies and distortions. Distortions left unchecked do not resolve themselves over time; they must be identified and addressed. I know this from personal experience.

In 2014, I reached a state of burnout that affected my leadership and ministry effectiveness as a senior pastor, and the staff of pastors I served with and the board of elders decided it was time for me to leave. After serving faithfully with them for over ten years—I had done nothing immoral to disqualify myself from ministry—I was shocked by their lack of support and unwillingness to help me work things out. After less than three months of meetings, all but one elder (who resigned in protest) called for my resignation. I refused to resign, partly because I was not willing to let the congregation believe my resignation was a mutual decision between myself and the elders. I was also unwilling to imply that God was calling me out of the church into another ministry. In response, the elders immediately terminated my employment.

I was devastated and deeply hurt. I felt betrayed by men who I thought were my friends. I was under the illusion that we were a family, committed to working things out in an amicable way. As I walked out of the church building the night I was terminated, I asked, "God, why is this happening? What am I going to do now? How am I going to tell my wife when I get home?" I was filled with confusion and had never felt more rejected, abandoned, and hurt.

I didn't realize it at the time, but how I processed that traumatic situation was greatly influenced by unresolved emotional pain and former distortions I still had from past experiences. The torrent of unresolved pain made the fresh pain a hundred times worse.

In the days that followed, it felt like I was unraveling emotionally, and I knew I needed more help than my family and friends could give. So I sought out professional help from Dr. Bill Gaultiere, a psychologist and pastor who specializes in helping local church leaders.[7]

Early on in my therapy, Dr. Gaultiere asked me how I was feeling. My response was pretty raw: "I feel betrayed and victimized. The picture I have in my head is that I'm riding in the car with my friends, and suddenly, one turns on me with a gun and shoots me in the head, another opens the door and pushes me out into the street, and they all drive off, leaving me alone in the gutter to die." I was angry, but underneath it all was an overwhelming feeling of failure: I failed God, my family, the congregation I loved, my staff, and the elders I served with. I was stuck in an abyss of shame and consumed with the terror of an uncertain future, perhaps long-term unemployment and financial disaster. I was catastrophizing everything. It felt like my life was over and my job prospects were bleak: Getting fired as a senior pastor doesn't look good on a résumé. Most search committees prefer a candidate with less baggage than I had, and I can't blame them. After twenty-five years as a local church pastor, I had become another casualty of a local church-ministry conflict. I was grieving the death of a dream.

These raw feelings were given extra weight by lies and distortions that went back to many of my early childhood experiences, such as my parents' divorce, which had promoted feelings of being unloved, unimportant, and abandoned. The incessant bullying and rejection by my peers I had experienced throughout elementary school was informing how I processed the experience of being terminated. These unresolved feelings and resurrected distorted thoughts were triggered by being fired. I felt I was unworthy of love and that I didn't really matter. During those early months of therapy, it became clear that I had a lot of baggage to unpack.

Early one morning a few months after my termination, I was sitting alone on the beach, near my house. It was still dark, and I was crying out to the Lord, feeling desperate about my situation and wondering what in the world I was going to do now. While sitting there, feeling like I was drowning in fear and sadness, God spoke to me. I didn't hear an audible voice, but I knew it was God because I would never make up what I heard in my head: "Ken, I want you to initiate a reconciliation process with the elders."

I couldn't believe what I was hearing. "What? Are you kidding me, God? Are you serious? The elders hurt *me*. They need to apologize to *me*. They need to go on a forgiveness tour for *me* and for everyone else they nuked by their decision."

Have you ever been there with God? Have you ever experienced something so painful, so grave that it caused you to lash out at the one who knows your situation and loves you the most? If you have, you know exactly what I'm talking about, for we have wrestled with God.

The longer I sat there on the beach and thought about what God was inviting me to do, the more I knew that he was right. I'll admit that I didn't do it with the best attitude, but I took out my cell phone and composed a text to each elder personally, asking if he would meet me for coffee. I made it clear that my only intention to meet was to apologize for my part in the process that lead to my termination. The texts were a simple act of humble obedience that brought about results that only God could bring about.

Over the next several months, I met with each elder and offered a heartfelt apology. One thing I discovered is that there is no downside to humility.[8] I could have easily stayed stuck in victim mode, allowing anger and bitterness to reside in my heart, but by God's grace, that's not what I did. Instead, I let God's desire for unity flow through me.

Reconciling with fellow believers who have hurt you doesn't make what they did okay, nor does it mean you have to vacation together or be golf buddies. But we must love one another as Christ has loved us: When we hurt each other or hold a grievance of any kind, we must apologize and do everything we can to right the wrong. This isn't only for the sake of unity but also for our own spiritual/emotional well-being.

A few months after my meetings with each elder, the board invited me to join them for a reconciliation service at the church. During the packed service, the cochairman made a public apology to me, my family, and the congregation. The apology was heartfelt and greatly appreciated. I preached my last sermon on the same topic I chose for my first sermon to the congregation ten years earlier: grace. And during the message, I offered my own heartfelt apology to the board and congregation as well. The service ended with Communion and a lot of tears.

Not long after the service, the cochairman and I sat down together with Dr. Bill Gaultiere and told the story, on camera, about the painful process that led up to my termination and the things we learned along the way about the nature of forgiveness and the importance of a better process when staffing changes need to happen in a church. The video was posted on Facebook and has brought healing and hope to many pastors, elder boards, and congregations who have endured similar difficulties.[9]

The story of my ministry burnout is an example of how unresolved emotional pain resulting from past experiences can be triggered by a current event and create a blast radius that hurts many people and presents a poor testimony to a watching world. The feelings of rejection, abandonment, fear, and shame that I experienced during my early childhood and teenage years informed a worldview with lies and distorted thoughts that I projected onto my termination experience, making it much more painful—for everyone involved—than it needed to be. Today, research supports the fact that many of the difficult situations we find ourselves in are caused by or made far worse by unresolved emotional pain that distorts our thinking, creates distress, and leads to destructive behavior.[10]

The Correlation between Distorted Thoughts and Damaging Emotions

Dr. Caroline Leaf, a cognitive neuroscientist, explains the strong correlation between distorted thoughts and damaging emotions:

> Science shows that our thoughts, with their embedded feelings, turn sets of genes on and off in complex relationships. We take facts, experiences, and the events of life, and assign meaning to them with our thinking. . . .
>
> Our thoughts produce words and behaviors, which in turn stimulate more thinking and choices that build more thoughts in an endless cycle.

We are constantly reacting to circumstances and events, and as this cycle goes on, our brains become shaped by the process in either a positive, good-quality-of-life direction or a negative, toxic, poor-quality-of-life direction.[11]

According to Leaf, there is a cause-and-effect relationship between how a person chooses to think about a painful experience and the emotions that follow. Psychiatrist Curt Thompson agrees: "Virtually everything that we experience is shaped and influenced by emotional tone. . . . Whenever we are thinking or sensing something, emotion is part of the process."[12] These experts bear witness to the fact that thoughts beget feelings. For that set of feelings produced by our conscious thoughts, healthy thinking promotes healthy feelings (including love, joy, peace, hope, and gratitude), and unhealthy thinking—influenced by lies and distortions—promotes unhealthy feelings (including shame, fear, anger, depression, and anxiety).

While it's true that we cannot control our emotions directly, we can influence them indirectly by truth. What we want are feelings created by truth, not deception. In a very real sense, our beliefs and corresponding thoughts have a direct impact on the quality of our life. Philosopher and professor J. P. Moreland writes,

> Beliefs are the rails upon which our lives run. We almost always act according to what we really believe. . . . The actual content of what we believe about God, morality, politics, life after death, and so on will shape the contours of our lives and actions.[13]

A painful experience—like my termination—can both shape and expose the beliefs and thoughts inherent in a faulty worldview. A worldview shaped by lies distorts reality, leading to damaging thoughts and feelings that influence the will toward sinful behavior. Sinful behavior, then, is often less an act of outright rebellion against God and more a distorted, damaged attempt to cope with or numb emotional pain.

Regardless of the cause, sin quenches and hinders the work of the Spirit in Christ-formation and thus a more complete experience of the abundant life. To stop this destructive cycle, we must expose the lies and neutralize the shame.

Restoring My Soul with God

We are all prone to distorted perceptions about God. In order to replace these lies, we must internalize the truth about God as revealed to us in Scripture. Psalm 86 is a helpful place to start. For the next three days, spend ten minutes a day reflecting on Psalm 86 using the following questions as a guide.

DAY 1: Read Psalm 86 from your favorite translation three times and make a list below of the character traits David attributes to God.

_____

_____

_____

DAY 2: Read Psalm 86. This time, make a list of David's requests and reference his attitude before the Lord.

_____

_____

_____

DAY 3: Write out Psalm 86:15 on a 3 × 5 card and read it twice a day—once in the morning, when you first wake up, and again in the evening, right before you fall asleep. Do this exercise for seven consecutive days.

Restoring My Soul with Others

1. Why is it common for people to think that God is always angry? How could you help them reconcile this distortion?

2. What distortions about God can you identify in yourself?

3. Why is our view of God so important to Christ-formation and abundant living?

4. If you feel comfortable doing so, share a painful life experience that shaped your worldview. Can you identify any conflicts those experiences created? Any distortions about God? Any distortions about yourself? How have you processed the pain from those past experiences?

5. In your own words, explain the correlation between distorted thoughts and damaging emotions. Give an example of a distorted thought and an example of a corresponding emotion.

7

THE DECEPTIVE POWER
OF SHAME

A DISTORTED WORLDVIEW IS COMPOSED of beliefs that attach themselves to our conscious thoughts and influence how we think about various life experiences. These messages produce any number of unhealthy emotions, most profoundly (and most elementally) the totalizing experience of shame. The lies empowered by toxic shame are corrected by what the Bible says is true about God, self, and others, but until they are confronted with this revelation, they retain their deceptive power. This is why shame, from the very beginning, has stood so firmly between human beings and their Creator.

Toxic shame condemns and rejects using lies about identity and worth. We are not speaking here about healthy, corrective shame regulation in the brain's attachment system, which protects relationships. A little shot of shame is healthy, for example, after we are mean to someone we should love. Combined with truth, the little dose of shame-pain safeguards our cherished relationships. Healthy shame helps us learn to be our true selves—provided it comes with correction, not condemnation—and has an important function in our socialization and in improving our character.[1]

Jesus experienced shame without believing lies or accepting condemnation of himself (Hebrews 12:2). The apostle Paul uses healthy shame as a corrective (see 1 Corinthians 6:5; 15:34). He sees something wrong with people who do not feel healthy shame about sin (Philippians 3:19). Charles Manson, by contrast, diligently removed healthy shame from his followers so that they would mate, kill, and steal without remorse.[2] What we are discussing in this book is the toxic shame that comes from false beliefs.

Shame Damages the Heart

Shame researcher Brené Brown maintains that "shame is a core emotion—it strikes us at our center and radiates through every part of us."[3] Sociologist Thomas J. Scheff argues that "shame is the master emotion of everyday life."[4] Psychiatrist Curt Thompson takes it a step further, referring to shame as "evil in its most fundamental mode of operation."[5] Shame is deceptive and powerful and is perhaps Satan's most effective weapon for spiritual warfare.

Shame produces feelings of unworthiness. Psychologists Wilkie Au and Noreen Canon Au write, "Shame is rooted in a deep-seated fear that we are flawed, inadequate, and unworthy of love."[6] The fear produced by shame is the fear of disconnection. Brown explains,

> Shame is all about fear. . . . When we are experiencing shame, we are steeped in the fear of being ridiculed, diminished or seen as flawed. We are afraid that we've exposed or revealed a part of us that jeopardizes our connection and our worthiness of acceptance.[7]

Scientists have determined that both emotional pain and physical pain are processed in the same area of the brain. In other words, pain is pain regardless of whether it is a broken leg or a broken heart.[8]

How Shame Produces Fear

Shame and the fear of disconnection produce a stress response in the body that causes the brain to release toxic levels of adrenaline and cortisol into the bloodstream, producing biochemical reactions that adversely affect emotional and physical wellness. Caroline Leaf explains,

When cortisol and adrenalin are allowed to race unchecked through the body, they begin to have adverse effects on the cardiovascular system causing high blood pressure, heart palpitations and even aneurysms or strokes. . . . Next, the cortisol bathes the brain's nerve cells causing memories to literally shrink, affecting the ability to remember and think creatively. This destructive path continues until the body begins to suffer total system breakdown, leading to an emotional black hole, creeping illness and even premature death.[9]

Based on Leaf's findings, distorted thinking causes emotional and physical damage to the body. Shame affects both aspects of the human soul: material and immaterial. The stress response produced by shame and fear directly affects our capacity to experience the abundant life.

We are adversely affected by the fear of disconnection because we cannot thrive alone: God created us to need the love we can only experience in relationships. Anything that jeopardizes our connection with God and others triggers a stress response in the brain. Sadly, shame begets more shame and inhibits the very relationships people need in order to thrive. Curt Thompson explains,

As it turns out, humans tend to experience no greater distress than when in relationships of intentional, unqualified abandonment—abandoned physically and left out of the mind of the other. With shame, I not only sense that something is deeply wrong with me, but accompanying this is the naturally extended consequence that because of this profound flaw, you will eventually want nothing to do with me and will leave. Paradoxically, then, shame is a leveraging affect that anticipates abandonment while simultaneously initiating movement away—leaving.[10]

Shame and the fear of disconnection create such a high level of emotional distress that we will do almost anything to escape it, including turning to addictions to numb the pain. But there is good news here.

Neuroscientists have determined that what we choose to think about can change the negative bias of the brain. In other words, God has given us the ability to rewire our brain by identifying and replacing deeply imbedded, distorted thoughts with new thoughts based on biblical truth. In the same way that negative and distorted thoughts produce toxic emotions, biblically informed thoughts promote life and health.

In the next chapter, I will discuss findings from neuroscience that help us understand how and why our thoughts have such a powerful effect on our Christ-formation. The change is due in part to the pliable nature of the brain that neuroscientists refer to as *neuroplasticity*.

Restoring My Soul with God

1. Choose from the list below any words you would use to complete this sentence: "I am not _____ enough."

   - good-looking
   - good
   - strong

   - smart
   - talented
   - graceful

2. These "not enough" words are distortions and signs of shame. Choose and reflect on a passage below to help rewire these shame-producing thoughts with God's truth:

   You made all the delicate, inner parts of my body and knit them together in my mother's womb. Thank you for making me so wonderfully complex! It is amazing to think about. Your *workmanship* is marvelous—and how well I know it. You were there while I was being formed in utter seclusion! You saw me before I was born and scheduled each day of my life before I began to breathe. Every day was recorded in your book!

   How precious it is, Lord, to realize that you are thinking about me constantly! I can't even count how many times a day your thoughts turn toward me. And when I waken in the morning, you are still thinking of me!

   PSALM 139:13-18, TLB

God made the only one who did not know sin to become sin for us, so that we who did not know righteousness might become the righteousness of God through our union with him.

2 CORINTHIANS 5:21, TPT

Don't let your hearts be troubled. Trust in God, and trust also in me. There is more than enough room in my Father's home. If this were not so, would I have told you that I am going to prepare a place for you? When everything is ready, I will come and get you, so that you will always be with me where I am.

JOHN 14:1-3, NLT

He handed out gifts above and below, filled heaven with his gifts, filled earth with his gifts. He handed out gifts of apostle, prophet, evangelist, and pastor-teacher to train Christ's followers in skilled servant work, working within Christ's body, the church, until we're all moving rhythmically and easily with each other, efficient and graceful in response to God's Son, fully mature adults, fully developed within and without, fully alive like Christ.

EPHESIANS 4:10-13, MSG

The Spirit you received does not make you slaves, so that you live in fear again; rather, the Spirit you received brought about your adoption to sonship. And by him we cry, "*Abba*, Father." The Spirit himself testifies with our spirit that we are God's children. Now if we are children, then we are heirs—heirs of God and coheirs with Christ, if indeed we share in his sufferings in order that we may also share in his glory.

ROMANS 8:15-17, NIV

Restoring My Soul with Others

1. Discuss your shame word(s) from above and share the verse(s) that helped you rewire that thought. Describe the experience.

2. How would you explain shame to someone?

3. Read Genesis 3:6-13 and discuss your thoughts about the cause and effects of shame:

> When the woman saw that the tree was good for food, and that it was a delight to the eyes, and that the tree was to be desired to make one wise, she took of its fruit and ate, and she also gave some to her husband who was with her, and he ate. Then the eyes of both were opened, and they knew that they were naked. And they sewed fig leaves together and made themselves loincloths.
>
> And they heard the sound of the Lord God walking in the garden in the cool of the day, and the man and his wife hid themselves from the presence of the Lord God among the trees of the garden. But the Lord God called to the man and said to him, "Where are you?" And he said, "I heard the sound of you in the garden, and I was afraid, because I was naked, and I hid myself." He said, "Who told you that you were naked? Have you eaten of the tree of which I commanded you not to eat?" The man said, "The woman whom you gave to be with me, she gave me fruit of the tree, and I ate." Then the Lord God said to the woman, "What is this that you have done?" The woman said, "The serpent deceived me, and I ate."

4. Why do you think shame is so powerful?

5. Does it surprise you that physical and emotional pain register in the same part of the brain? Does this finding validate emotional pain? Discuss.

6. What causes you to feel stressed? Why is long-term stress so damaging to your body? What are some ways you could better deal with stressful situations?

8

HOW NEUROSCIENCE INFORMS CHRIST-FORMATION

OF ALL THE DYNAMICS OF THE HEART, the one you have the most ability to control is your thoughts. God has given us free will to choose what we will think about. This is important because thoughts have a direct effect on feelings and the choices you make. For example, if you allow Satan's lies to inform your thinking, you will experience toxic emotions, including shame and fear. But if you choose God's truth to inform your thinking, you will experience healthy emotions, including peace (Isaiah 26:3) and joy (Psalm 16:8-9). Findings from neuroscience help us understand the power of thoughts, and this information will better inform us about Christ-formation and abundant living.

What Can Neuroscience Teach Me about Christ-Formation?

As recent as twenty years ago, neuroscientists believed that the brain's capacity to change was fixed by somewhere between ten and nineteen years of age. More recent studies aided by more advanced brain-scanning technology have changed this former thinking. Today, it is commonly understood that the brain can change throughout a person's life. It's true that the brain's capacity for change slows down with age because thinking patterns become stronger over time through years of repetition, but change is possible: You actually *can* teach an old dog new tricks.

James Zull, director of the University Center for Innovation in Teaching and Education at Case Western Reserve University, explains the brain's ability to change using the analogy of silly putty:

> Like a piece of silly putty, the brain is molded and reshaped by the forces of life acting on it. Our wiring grows and develops depending on what we experience—even before birth. As we interact with the world, the world becomes internalized, or mapped, in our brain. The extensive plasticity of the brain continues throughout life.[1]

Several different forces influence the way we think about things. The most important include: (1) family of origin, (2) society and culture, (3) painful life experiences, and (4) church background.

Family of Origin and Early Childhood Experiences

As children, we don't have the capacity to accurately understand hurtful experiences. For example, a father trips over his little boy's toys and yells at his son: "How many times do I have to tell you to pick up your toys?" It turns out the father had a really bad day at work—at least some of the anger in his tone is related to his work frustrations. The little boy doesn't know this; he would experience shame for being yelled at (but would not understand why). Every parent loses their temper at times and can say hurtful things in a moment of frustration. In doing so, they unintentionally hurt their children. Lack of intent to cause harm does not mitigate the pain.

When children get hurt early in life, they often carry that pain for the rest of their life. Consider the studies done with orphans in Romania following the collapse of Communism there. The economy declined throughout the entire Eastern Bloc region, leaving over one hundred thousand children orphaned in overcrowded government institutions. All the basic needs of each child were provided—they were changed, kept warm, and fed—but due to fear of spreading germs and disease, these children received limited attention in the way of cuddling, hugs, and other appropriate displays of affection.

This lack of touch had a devastating impact on the children. Years later, after these orphaned children became adults, many of them volunteered for testing to determine how their early childhood experiences affected them. The brains of these grown-up orphans were found to be smaller in size and lower in brain activity than children raised in more favorable circumstances. This study and those like it reveal that early childhood distress can damage the brain.

Children need a lot of affirmation and affection in order to thrive and develop properly. Journalist Vivian Giang argues that

> Your ability to maintain proper social skills and develop a sense of empathy is largely dependent on the physical affection, eye contact, and playtime of those early years. Even something as simple as observing facial expressions and understanding what those expressions mean is tied to your wellbeing as a toddler.[2]

The brain changes with the onset of new experiences and thoughts. And because the aspects of the heart affect each other, whatever you choose to think about will affect your capacity to experience the love you need in order to thrive. Caroline Leaf understands the negative impact distorted thinking has on the heart:

> Thoughts stimulate emotions which then result in attitude and finally produce behavior. This symphony of electrochemical reactions in the body affects the way we think and feel physically. Therefore, toxic thoughts produce toxic emotions, which produce toxic attitudes, resulting in toxic behavior.[3]

A "toxic thought" is a negative or distorted thought that produces emotional distress. Many toxic thoughts are introduced early in life through distressing experiences within the family, neighborhood, school, or extracurricular activities. If left unattended, these thoughts will linger in the heart and contribute to the spiritual/emotional conflicts that hinder Christ-formation.

Culture and Ethnicity

Cultural neuroscientists investigate how the values of a particular culture affect the brain, specifically the way a person thinks about and perceives reality. For example, the heart of a child born and raised in the United States, Canada, or Europe will be shaped by the values inherent in those cultures, including individualism, personal uniqueness, and independence. Social scientists refer to these values as *radical individualism*. Joseph Hellerman explains,

> We in America have been socialized to believe that our own dreams, goals, and personal fulfillment ought to take precedence over the well-being of any group—our church or our family, for example—to which we belong. The immediate needs of the individual are more important than the long-term health of the group. . . .
>
> Our culture has powerfully socialized us to believe that personal happiness and fulfillment should take precedence over the connections we have with others in both our families and our churches.[4]

The individualistic worldview to which Hellerman refers is most common in Western culture; nearly all other societies adhere to a value system that is more relational and group oriented. For example, Asian, African, and Indian cultures promote a more collective, familial, and interdependent set of values. Regardless of the cultural values you prefer, cultural scripts and practices shape the heart and promote thoughts and feelings that are culturally preferred.[5]

Painful Life Experiences

Painful experiences negatively shape the heart, but some cause more distress than others. Whether the pain is caused by immediate family members, loved ones, friends, coworkers, a personal failure, a forced termination from a job, or a victimizing event (such as assault, rape, or robbery), emotional pain is real and can be as debilitating as physical pain.

We must not overlook how emotional pain affects our discipleship to Jesus. Pastor and author Peter Scazzero argues,

> Somehow, today we slice out the emotional portion of who we are, deeming it suspect, irrelevant, or of secondary importance.

Contemporary discipleship models often esteem the spiritual more than the physical, emotional, social, and intellectual components of who we are. Nowhere, however, does a good biblical theology support such a division.[6]

All aspects of our personhood affect each other; that is why Christ-formation must be considered a holistic process. Therefore, we must include a means for healing damaged emotions in our understanding of discipleship.

Church Experiences

The fourth shaping factor of the heart includes a person's church background. If you grew up in a particular church or denomination, the culture of that congregation shaped the way you think about God, yourself, and others. The local church has a powerful effect on a person's worldview. You perceive God, yourself, and other people through that lens. This is especially true in regard to your concept of God. Pastor and author A. W. Tozer rightly pointed out that

> What comes into our minds when we think about God is the most important thing about us. . . .
>
> [T]he most portentous fact about any man is not what he at a given time may say or do, but what he in his deep heart conceives God to be like. We tend by a secret law of the soul to move toward our metal image of God. . . .
>
> I believe there is scarcely an error in doctrine or a failure in applying Christian ethics that cannot be traced finally to imperfect and ignoble thoughts about God.[7]

We will talk more about how to correct distorted thoughts about God in a later chapter, but for now, I want you to understand that your perception of God is critical to Christ-formation and your ability to experience the abundant life.

How We Wire (or Rewire) Our Brains

How you choose to think about and interpret the experiences you have had from within each of these four forces will affect your emotions and decision-making process and ultimately play out in your behavior. For example, I remember once when I was three or four years old, my parents set me outside the front door, during the night, while they had a serious argument. At the time, we lived in a house that was isolated down in a gully, so I couldn't see any neighbors or people walking around, and I was afraid of being alone in the dark. I remember hearing them yelling at each other through the door but not knowing why. *Did I do something bad? Was I being punished? Were they going to hurt each other?* All I knew was my mommy and daddy were yelling at each other, and I was very afraid. As I grew older, this memory faded but not the fear of the dark that has been with me until recently, when I was teaching at a men's retreat. I felt shame and embarrassment as I shared my fear, wondering if some of the guys would laugh or reject me. But in spite of these feelings, I thought it was an important story to tell. After the talk, my wife reminded me of that traumatic night I was placed outside in the dark, connecting the dots for me between that experience and my ongoing fear.

Susan's insight helped me reframe that experience. My parents didn't put me outside that night because they didn't love me, nor did they want to hurt me. Instead, they were trying to protect me from watching them fight. They were young and scared themselves and acted in a way that they thought was best in the heat of the moment.

Today I choose to think about that memory differently, and it promotes different emotions. I was never in any danger outside the house that night, my parents did not hurt each other physically, and I wasn't being punished for something bad I had done. Their fight had nothing to do with me. Due to this process of reframing, my fear of the dark is subsiding. Thinking differently about that situation didn't change the experience, but it did promote different feelings that are helping me experience a different quality of life.

The brain is composed of approximately one hundred billion interconnected neurons called gray matter. Neurons are cells that process and transmit information in the brain through synapses: bridges of electrical signals that connect neurons to each other and carry the transmitted messages. Neuroscientists maintain that there are enough neurons in the brain to store every experience you have ever had. In fact, according to researchers from the Salk Institute in La Jolla, California, the estimated capacity of the brain is a petabyte—a capacity equivalent to the entire World Wide Web.[8]

Neurons are birthed by thoughts. The more you think about something, the more neurons are developed around that thought, and the stronger and more influential that thought becomes. Remember, thoughts stimulate emotions, emotions affect decisions, and all these gears turning together drive behavior. This is why most of what we do can be traced back to thinking patterns.

This process may seem overly simplistic, but it's true. According to Leaf, positive, healthy thoughts produce new neurons, which in turn produce healthy emotions that affect the will and influence behavior. The same process applies to negative and distorted thinking. The longer you dwell on negative and distorted thoughts, the stronger and more toxic they become. Leaf continues,

> As the person relives the event over and over, it wires itself deeper into the mind, becoming a main filter and disrupting normal function. Flashbacks—reliving the bad memory many times a day—strengthen the circuit, making it worse and more debilitating.[9]

The point is, whatever you choose to dwell on wires your brain for either a positive or a negative response. Leaf concludes,

> As we think, we change the physical nature of our brain. As we consciously direct our thinking, we can wire out toxic patterns of thinking and replace them with healthy thoughts. New thought networks grow. . . .
> It all starts in the realm of the mind, with our ability to think and choose.[10]

In Matthew 6:25-34, Jesus tells us not to worry (a form of constant negative thinking). When we worry, we think about all the "what-ifs" that might happen. *What if I don't have enough to eat, or drink, or wear?* Worrying triggers a stress response in the brain that puts the body into a defensive posture known as "fight or flight"—a state of high alert where the brain is constantly scanning for danger. Needless to say, this does not put us into a state of joy and peace. Instead of letting us worry that we might not have enough to survive, Jesus tells us to learn a lesson from the birds: "Look at the birds of the air; they do not sow or reap or store away in barns, and yet your heavenly Father feeds them. Are you not much more valuable than they?" (Matthew 6:26, NIV). In other words, Jesus is saying, "Instead of worrying, put your faith into action by thinking about the loving care of your heavenly Father." Peter makes a similar point: "Give all your worries and cares to God, for he cares about you" (1 Peter 5:7, NLT). The power of thought can work *against* us, as in the example of worrying, or *for* us, as in the example of thinking about how loving and caring our heavenly Father is. You really can change your brain and quality of life by carefully choosing what you will think about.

Dr. Arne May of the Institute of Neuroradiology at the University of Regensburg observed the brain's ability to change by training college students how to juggle. During the juggling experiment, each student practiced a classic three-ball routine for three months. Brain scans were conducted on each student before and after the training. The experiment revealed significant neuron development in the area of the brain associated with juggling. Then subjects were asked to *not* practice the juggling routine for three months. A third brain scan revealed a significant reduction of neurons in the same area of the brain.[11] The implications of this experiment are important: Whatever we choose to focus our mind on consistently becomes dominant in our mind, directly influencing our feelings and behavior.

This helps us understand the correlation between thinking and Christ-formation. We can literally replace the lies and distorted thoughts that wreak havoc in our lives by replacing them with thinking that is aligned with the Bible. Focused attention on biblical truth results in freedom and abundance. Neuroplasticity can be self-directed by changing what we think about.

Doctors Jeffery Schwartz and Rebecca Gladding explain,

Neuroplasticity is operating all the time, which means that if you repeatedly engage in the same behaviors (even something as benign as checking your e-mail several times a day), neuroplasticity will designate that action as the preferred one, regardless of the effect of that behavior on you and your life. In a very real way, the actions you perform now and how you focus your attention have downstream effects on how your brain is wired and how you will automatically respond to deceptive brain messages and events in the future. Thus, for better or for worse, focused attention creates the brain you will live with.[12]

Schwartz and Gladding make an important point: Whatever thoughts we choose to think about over and over become a thought habit that can hijack the brain. Even if these thoughts cause us distress, the painful feelings will not be strong enough to change our thinking patterns. The thoughts we choose to dwell on become a figurative rut we get stuck in.

In order to better understand how this rut producing process works, we need to understand two important dynamics of neuroplasticity: Hebb's law and the quantum Zeno effect.

Why It's So Difficult to Break Bad Habits

In 1949, Canadian psychologist Donald Hebb published a theory that has become known as Hebb's law and can be summarized by the saying "Neurons that fire together, wire together."[13] The process is similar to what happens when you exercise by lifting weights. As you lift more weight over time, your muscles become stronger. In a similar way, when a person repeatedly engages in a thought or behavior, the neurons that develop from this thought or behavior become stronger, making that behavior the default routine. In other words, whatever you choose to consistently repeat—whether it is a thought or activity—creates a network of neurons. The more you think a specific thought or engage in a specific behavior, the more robust that network of neurons becomes.

This is how we form habits, by doing the same thing over and over. Norman Doidge uses the example of a child learning the alphabet to explain Hebb's law:

As a child learns the alphabet, the visual shape of the letter A is connected with the sound "ay." Each time the child looks at the letter and repeats the sound, the neurons involved "fire together" at the same time, and then "wire together"; the synaptic connections between them are strengthened. Whenever any activity that links neurons is repeated, those neurons fire faster, stronger, sharper signals together, and the circuit gets more efficient and better at helping to perform the skill.[14]

Another way to understand Hebb's law is to picture multiple cars driving down a muddy road. The more cars that travel the same path, the deeper the ruts become. After the mud dries, it leaves behind deep ruts that are difficult to steer out of when you drive into them. The more you think a thought, the deeper the rut in the brain becomes, making it hard to stop thinking. This repeated focus of thinking has a term: the quantum Zeno effect.

The Superglue That Holds Negative Thoughts in Place

Think of the quantum Zeno effect as the superglue that holds a thought in place long enough for Hebb's law to take effect. The quantum Zeno effect is achieved by focused attention. Neuroscientists refer to this as "attention density." Schwartz and Gladding explain,

> [*attention density*:] *Repeatedly* focusing your attention on something (a thought, sensation, event, response, action) over and over. The more you sustain your focus of attention on something (i.e., the denser your attention is), the more likely a specific habit will be wired into your brain.
>
> In the brain, attention density is the first—and most important—step in creating strong, enduring brain circuits. Attention density makes the quantum Zeno effect "kick in" and causes focused attention to have powerful effects on the brain by activating Hebb's law....
>
> [A]ttention is what drives the quantum Zeno effect.[15]

Both aspects of neuroplasticity can either work *for* or *against* you. If you dwell on negative thoughts—like worrying about life necessities—those thoughts will grow stronger and add to your distressing emotions. The same is true if you choose to dwell on healthy, positive, and biblically informed thoughts. Here we can apply Isaiah 26:3: "You will keep in perfect peace all who trust in you, all whose thoughts are fixed on you!" (NLT). When you choose to stop dwelling on certain thoughts, those thoughts will dissipate over time.

Once I understood these two dynamics of neuroplasticity, I realized how important it was to meditate on and memorize Scripture: When I engage in this spiritual discipline, I can actually rewire my brain by exercising my free will to choose the thoughts I will think about. With this new understanding of neuroplasticity, I began to see more and more biblical evidence supporting what researchers have discovered: that our thoughts hold tremendous power. In the next chapter, I will share with you how this understanding of neuroplasticity can help you break free from past hurtful memories and the beliefs that cause painful emotions.

Restoring My Soul with God

Take as much time and paper as you need to work through the following questions:

1. What is the happiest memory from your childhood? Describe the situation in detail. What feelings come up for you now as you think about that time? What do you want to say to the Lord about that?

2. What is the most painful memory you have from elementary school? Now, imagine yourself sitting on Jesus' lap. What does he want to say to you about that situation?

3. Of the four forces that shape the heart, which had the greatest impact on your emotions? Was it okay to have emotions? Were your emotions ever validated?

4. Which family member took the greatest interest in your thoughts and feelings?

_____

_____

_____

5. If you grew up in church, how did the teaching and doctrine in your church shape your perspective of God?

_____

_____

_____

6. Pray, asking God to reveal any habits he wants you to deal with. What is he asking you to do? What have you learned from this chapter that can help you with the process to change?

_____

_____

_____

Restoring My Soul with Others

1. What is your biggest takeaway from this chapter?

2. How would you describe neuroplasticity (remember the silly putty example)?

3. According to Hebb's law ("neurons that fire together, wire together") and the quantum Zeno effect (practicing attention density), explain in your own words—as best as you can—what takes place in your brain when you worry.

4. How do these findings from neuroscience help you understand Christ-formation and how to experience abundant life? Discuss.

9

BREAKING FREE FROM
PAINFUL MEMORIES

THERE IS AN OLD SAYING THAT "time heals all wounds." The idea is that healing for damaged emotions as a result of traumatic or distressing events happens automatically with the passing of time. The truth, however, is that time alone heals nothing. No matter how much time goes by, unresolved emotional pain will not heal by itself; it must be identified (named) and processed (shared with others) accordingly. We will talk about how to heal unresolved emotional pain in a later chapter, but in this chapter, I want to show that according to Scripture, we must go back and resolve the pain from our past in order to move forward into the future.

To do this, we must first understand how memory works.

During the many years I've been a pastor, I've had people challenge the need to resolve past issues through counseling. To support their point, "no counseling" advocates often refer to Paul's words in Philippians 3:13-14: "One thing I do: forgetting what lies behind and straining forward to what lies ahead, I press on toward the goal for the prize of the upward call of God in Christ Jesus." At first glance, it may look like the "no counseling" advocates have a point: Paul seems to commend "forgetting what lies behind." In order to understand what Paul really means, we must look at the context.

Paul's entire discussion in Philippians 3 is a comparison of his former, self-directed righteousness according to the law with true righteousness that comes from God by faith in Jesus Christ.

> If anyone else thinks he has reason for confidence in the flesh,
> I have more: circumcised on the eighth day, of the people of
> Israel, of the tribe of Benjamin, a Hebrew of Hebrews; as to the
> law, a Pharisee; as to zeal, a persecutor of the church; as to
> righteousness under the law, blameless.
>
> PHILIPPIANS 3:4-6

Paul was a Pharisee who had worked rigorously to uphold the righteous requirements of the law. In fact, he was very proud of the fact that he was blameless (without any fault) in carrying out the letter of the law. The Mosaic law said, "You shall not murder" (Exodus 20:13). Paul never murdered anyone. The Mosaic law said, "You shall not commit adultery" (Exodus 20:14). Paul never committed adultery. The Mosaic law said, "You shall not bear false witness against your neighbor" (Exodus 20:16). Paul never did that either. According to carrying out the letter of the law, Paul was blameless. These acts of legalistic righteousness had been Paul's trophies, evidence that he was a good Jew, in right standing with God. In other words, before Paul met Jesus, he believed that his relationship with God was secure based on his good works.

And yet, after his conversion on the road to Damascus (Acts 9:1-19), Paul realized that all his good works accounted for nothing. In fact, he refers to his legalistic righteousness as "rubbish" (Philippians 3:8). The English word *rubbish* does not convey the graphic comparison Paul was making. The Greek word translated as "rubbish" here, *skybala*, is used in reference to various kinds of filth, including human excrement.[1] Paul is being intentionally graphic, maybe even offensive, in his choice of words, but he is making the point that human effort can never produce right standing before God; righteousness can only be received as a gift from God through faith in Jesus Christ (Philippians 3:9-10). By "forgetting what lies behind," therefore, Paul is not advocating that believers should just move on from the pain of their past; he is arguing that, theologically, his previous focus on religious achievement is irrelevant to his right standing with God.

Paul does not argue for us to forget past events. As you read Scripture, especially the Old Testament, you will discover that God wants his people to remember their history.

Remembering the Past Is Important to God

God is an eternal being, not limited by time and space. And yet, he remembers what he has done in the past. Consider the rainbow (Genesis 9:16) and the covenant God made with Abraham, Isaac, and Jacob (Leviticus 26:42). Not only does God pay attention to the past, he wants his people to as well. God commanded the Israelites to remember their time in Egypt, specifically, the fact that he delivered them from their bondage and oppression (Deuteronomy 5:15). God commanded his people to remember his faithfulness to them in the wilderness (Deuteronomy 8:2). Today, believers are encouraged to remember all that God has done for them as well (Psalms 77:11; 103:2).

In order to remember the past, God established feasts and festivals, including Passover, Pentecost (Festival of Weeks), Festival of Trumpets (Rosh Hashanah), Day of Atonement (Yom Kippur), and Festival of Shelters (Sukkot). God commanded the Israelites to set aside these times to remember his faithfulness to his people, making special note of God's protection, provision, and presence.

This emphasis on remembering also involved building altars. Throughout the Old Testament, an altar was a symbol to remind people about God's faithfulness. For example, after God appeared to Jacob at Bethel, he built an altar to remember the Lord (Genesis 28:18). Again, after God delivered Jacob from the hand of his brother, Esau, he built an altar to the Lord (Genesis 33:20; 35:1-3). After Israel defeated the Amalekites and after receiving the Ten Commandments, Moses built altars to the Lord (Exodus 17:14-15; 24:4). When God dried up the Jordan River so the Israelites could cross into the Promised Land, God commanded them to build an altar to remind future generations of what he had done for them (Joshua 4:1-9).

Various iterations of the word *remember* are found in forty-seven verses of twenty-eight chapters in nineteen books of the King James Version of the Bible.[2] Remembering past events is important because what we choose to think about regarding God's character and nature and our experiences affect the heart—and therefore our Christ-formation and the abundant life.

The meaning we attribute to a painful life experience can promote thoughts and emotions that distort our perception of God, self, and others.

As an example of how this works, let's compare Adam and Eve's experience before versus after the Fall. Prior to the Fall, Adam and Eve only experienced good; they had no experience of evil nor the fruit of sin, namely shame, fear, and eventual death. God commanded them not to eat from the tree of the knowledge of good and evil (Genesis 2:17) not out of selfish ambition or jealousy (to keep them from becoming like him, as Satan implied) but to protect them from harm. God did not want them to experience evil and the devastating consequences of sin.

Sadly, Eve was deceived and chose to believe Satan's lies instead of God's word. She ate of the fruit and gave some to Adam, who ate of it too. Then "the eyes of both were opened, and they knew that they were naked. And they sewed fig leaves together and made themselves loincloths" (Genesis 3:7). Sin distorted how Adam and Eve thought about nakedness and each other. No longer was the vulnerability of nakedness good, but something to fear and be ashamed of.

Sin also changed the way they thought about God. Before the Fall, the only thoughts they had of God were good: He was a loving creator who placed them in a beautiful garden and provided everything they needed in abundance (Genesis 2:8-9). Sin changed how they thought about God. Love for God was replaced with the fear of God:

> They heard the sound of the LORD God walking in the garden in
> the cool of the day, and the man and his wife hid themselves from
> the presence of the LORD God among the trees of the garden. But
> the LORD God called to the man and said to him, "Where are
> you?" And he said, "I heard the sound of you in the garden, and I
> was afraid, because I was naked, and I hid myself."
> GENESIS 3:8-10

Sin birthed the feelings of fear and shame that distorted Adam and Eve's perception of God, self, and each other. Now, instead of living naked and unashamed (Genesis 2:25), they tried to hide their shame, weakness, and vulnerability behind a fig-leaf mask. And the same is true for us today.

Whenever you encounter sin, whether your own or a sin committed against you, you will experience shame and fear that can affect your perception about God, self, and others. For example, say you're walking through Central Park in New York City on a beautiful summer evening. It's late and there are few people around, but you feel safe and it's such a beautiful night, so you keep walking. Suddenly from behind the trees along the path, a masked man with a gun jumps out and demands your wallet. You realize you're in mortal danger and freeze. Instead of waiting for you to pull out your wallet, the man hits you in the head with his gun, almost knocking you out. While lying on the ground, dazed and confused, he forcefully grabs your wallet and runs. As you lie there in pain, you realize you have been violently assaulted and robbed. Thankfully, the thief didn't take your cell phone, so you call 911 for help.

The next day, as the shock begins to subside, you start to rehearse the events of the attack. The physical pain from this traumatic experience is bad enough, but now you start to berate yourself with thoughts like *You're so stupid, what were you thinking?* and *This whole thing is your fault; you should never have been walking alone at night.* You might even begin to have doubts about God: *Where was God in all this? Why didn't he protect me? If God loved me, he would never have allowed that to happen.* A traumatic event like this could make you distrustful of other people, causing you to fear a stranger walking toward you.

Instead of beating yourself up and entertaining doubts about God, you could reframe your experience by thinking, *I could have been more careful, but it seemed safe; there were other people around.* Or, *The thief is the bad guy here, not me: I was just in the wrong place at the wrong time.* You could also remember that Jesus never promised us a pain-free life, but he did promise to always be with us and to give us the strength to endure all things. The assault was a painful experience, both physically and emotionally, but how you choose to process the event will determine how much more pain you will experience as a result.

How we process an experience gets stored in our conscious and nonconscious memory and will largely determine the extent of toxic emotions or helpful emotions. So much of it depends on what we choose to think about.

Understanding the Nonconscious Mind

Memories contain both thoughts and corresponding emotions. Caroline Leaf writes, "Every time you build a memory, you activate emotion. . . .

Memory and emotions, like body and mind, are inseparable."[3] The brain stores the memories of all your experiences and their corresponding emotions in billions of interconnected neurons. Most of them, however, are not readily accessible. Daniel Siegel, clinical professor of psychiatry at the UCLA School of Medicine, argues, "Much of what occurs within our neural, relational, and mental lives is not within the experience of awareness."[4] Neuroscientists maintain that less than 0.1 percent of a person's thoughts are accessible at any one time. In other words, we are not aware of how most of the thoughts and emotions stored in our memory affect us. Leaf argues,

> The nonconscious mind is where 99.9 percent of our mind activity
> is. It is the root level that stores the thoughts with the emotions
> and perceptions, and it impacts the conscious mind and what we
> say and do.[5]

Most of the thoughts that drive our behavior emanate from our nonconscious mind—a deep place in the heart that holds our true motivations that only God knows (1 Kings 8:39; Psalm 44:21) (see Figure 9.1).

FIGURE 9.1

BEHAVIOR

EXPLICIT MEMORY

CONSCIOUS 0.1%

BEHAVIOR

IMPLICIT MEMORY

NONCONSCIOUS 99.9%

The Bible indicates that the human heart—the immaterial part of the self—is deep and that only God knows the thoughts and emotions therein. Consider the following verses:

- "The purpose in a man's heart is like deep water" (Proverbs 20:5).
- "He knows the secrets of the heart" (Psalm 44:21).
- "You alone know each human heart" (2 Chronicles 6:30, NLT).
- "Lord, you know everyone's heart" (Acts 1:24; see also Acts 15:8, NIV).
- "Man looks on the outward appearance, but the LORD looks on the heart" (1 Samuel 16:7).

Neuroscientists refer to the deep places of the heart as "the nonconscious mind." It is the repository of past thoughts, emotions, and perceptions that make up memories. Even though these are beyond awareness, they affect the conscious mind and influence what we say and do. Robert Saucy rightly pointed this out: "Simply stated, the deeper something is in our heart, the more it influences our life."[6] The thoughts and emotions that exist in the nonconscious do not dissipate over time but linger, and if they are toxic, they can leave us feeling overwhelmed and disconnected.

Buried emotions are buried alive but are prone to being triggered by a current experience. In his book *Rewire*, Richard O'Conner refers to the nonconscious mind as

> The repository of the repressed, the hidden truths about ourselves we don't want to face, the use of defenses like denial to help us not see uncomfortable reality. This is the part that contains all the feelings and thoughts we don't want to be conscious of. . . . The feelings we repress—fear, anger, guilt, shame, and others—can have pervasive effects throughout the automatic self. That repression distorts how we see reality and influences our feelings and our behavior in ways we can't begin to see. . . .
>
> When our feelings are in conflict with each other, or are unacceptable to us, we use defense mechanisms like denial and rationalization to put them into the unconscious part of our minds.[7]

Therefore, most of the thoughts, emotions, and perceptions that contribute to the spiritual/emotional conflicts that hinder Christ-formation and the abundant life reside in the nonconscious area of the heart. Robert Saucy explained it this way:

One of the greatest hindrances to our healing and growth is leaving the issues that trouble our life and stifle our transformation hidden and unknown in the depth of our heart, split off from our conscious thought. *So long as we think that we believe something, but the real thought in the depth of our heart is different, we will never experience personal transformation. . . .*

An honest appraisal of our spiritual condition—and that means the condition of our heart—is absolutely necessary for spiritual health and growth.[8]

In order to access and process the hurts in the deep places of the heart, it helps to have a basic understanding of how memory works.

How Memory Works

Picture the two rails on a railroad track as an illustration for how memory works. One rail symbolizes implicit memory, and the other rail symbolizes explicit memory. The two memory systems work side by side. One is not more important than another, but they encode different aspects of the same experience.

Explicit memory—also referred to as episodic memory—encodes the details of an experience. According to Daniel Schacter, professor of psychology at Harvard University, the episodic memory system "allows us explicitly to recall the personal incidents that uniquely define our lives."[9] When you are describing your last vacation to a friend—the sights, sounds, and smells; the food you ate; and the people you talked to—you are accessing explicit memory. Explicit memory is conscious—a fact that will be addressed in detail in a later chapter. Whenever you are aware that you are remembering something, you are accessing explicit memory.

As important as it is to understand how explicit memory works, it's equally important to understand how implicit memory works because a high percentage of the thoughts, emotions, and perceptions that hinder Christ-formation and the abundant life reside therein.

The implicit memory system resides in the nonconscious, that deep place in the heart that is beyond awareness for several reasons: Some processes are too deep in the brain, some run faster than conscious thinking, and others are much slower than what we usually notice. It will be helpful to associate implicit memory with the phrase *gut-awareness*. I'm sure you've had the common experience where you believed something was true but didn't have any hard facts to back it up; you just knew it in your gut. Theologian John Coe and psychologist Todd Hall provide a helpful explanation:

> Gut-level memory is not verbal; it is not memory of facts that can only be captured in words, or of events in our life that we can consciously (explicitly) recall. Instead, this kind of memory is recorded and packaged in a different "language" or "code" than words—it is recorded in our emotions, perceptions, bodily sensations and our body's "readiness" to respond in certain ways.[10]

The thoughts, emotions, and perceptions that reside in "gut-level" memory can be triggered unexpectedly by a current event. For example, imagine that, as a sixteen-year-old, you were in a serious car accident while driving a group of friends to the beach. The accident was not your fault, yet two of your friends died and you ended up in the hospital with life-threatening injuries. You spent months in physical therapy and psychotherapy as you tried to work through the guilt and depression resulting from the accident. Now, fast-forward twenty years. You're driving on the freeway with your wife sitting next to you and your three kids sitting in the back seats. And even though you haven't thought about that teenage accident for years, when the guy next to you cuts you off, you go into an immediate, homicidal rage. Now, you start tailgating that "jerk," putting the same people at risk you were trying to protect moments before. Emotionally and physically, your response doesn't make rational sense. You're having a completely disproportionate response to the situation.

What's going on? Could it be that, even though you hadn't thought about that teenage car accident in decades, you have been carrying the pain and guilt in your implicit memory and it was triggered by a careless driver? Painful thoughts, emotions, and perceptions, which are stored in implicit memory, can burst into the present in dramatic, even dangerous ways if they haven't been processed appropriately. Whenever you have a disproportionate reaction to a current event, it's very likely that an underlying thought, emotion, or perception is being triggered. If you don't pay attention to these experiences by addressing the underlying cause, they can negatively impact your life and the lives of those around you.

Both explicit and implicit memory systems affect the limbic system in the brain, the area largely responsible for processing emotion. Every thought has a corresponding emotion and perception, which releases a chemical messenger in the body produced by the hypothalamus. Leaf explains,

> What you think and feel prompts your hypothalamus to begin a series of chemical secretions that change the way you function. . . . the hypothalamus gland is actually the facilitator and originator of emotions in response to life circumstances, such as fear, anxiety, stress, tension, panic attacks, phobia, rage, anger and aggression.[11]

Thought, emotion, and perception prompt adrenaline, cortisol, and dopamine to be released into the brain. These, in turn, influence the will—the decision-making gear in the heart—and promote different types of behavior.

Now that we have explored the conscious and nonconscious aspects of the heart and the two types of memory (explicit and implicit), we can better understand why God wants his people to remember the past. Human behavior is complex, and there is a lot going on in the deep places of the heart. When painful memories stored in the nonconscious are triggered by current experiences, they can produce a chain reaction of negative thoughts and emotions that distort our perception and drive sinful behavior. God wants us to do the hard work of confronting those nonconscious memories that influence our current behavior—to make those connections between our irrational behavior (such as the road-rage example) and the implicit memories that inform them (like the emotions associated with the teenage car accident)—so they can be healed and transformed, so we can experience the abundant life.

The way to resolve the root problem underlying the spiritual/emotional conflicts that hinder Christ-formation and the abundant life is to rewire the brain with healthy, biblically informed thoughts. In the next chapter, I will show you how this process works.

Restoring My Soul with God

It can be scary to think about working through painful past experiences, but as you have learned in this chapter, pain doesn't disappear over time. For the next

five days, take twenty minutes each day to work through the following questions, asking God to reveal any deep hurts that might be hidden in your heart.

Read Psalm 139:1-6 (NLT) each day before taking the steps below.

O LORD, you have examined my heart
　　and know everything about me.
You know when I sit down or stand up.
　　You know my thoughts even when I'm far away.
You see me when I travel
　　and when I rest at home.
　　You know everything I do.
You know what I am going to say
　　even before I say it, LORD.
You go before me and follow me.
　　You place your hand of blessing on my head.
Such knowledge is too wonderful for me,
　　too great for me to understand!

1. Ask the Lord to search your heart and reveal any hurtful memories he
   wants to reveal to you. Write down the memory in a conversational
   way, being as detailed as you can. If you have difficulty, think about
   one of the examples you wrote down on your lifeline for the exercise
   after chapter 1. Tell the Lord you are having difficulty and ask him
   to help you. (*Example:* "Lord, I remember when Slim used to tease
   me in middle school when I lived in Utah. He used to call me 'prune
   picker,' and all the kids would laugh at me. I felt so sad and alone.
   I didn't feel like I had any friends. I felt rejected, like I didn't even
   matter to anyone.")

   _____

   _____

   _____

2. Now, ask the Lord what he wants to say to you about that situation.
   (*Example:* "Oh, Kenny, I was with you every time Slim teased you.
   I heard his hurtful words, and I saw your broken heart. I have kept

every tear in my bottle and written down every situation in my book. I, too, know what it's like to be despised and rejected. I love you. I'm so sorry that you were bullied and that kids would laugh at you. I want you to remember that you matter to me. I gave my life for you because I love you so much. I died so you can live. Come to me, and sit on my lap. Lean your head against my chest, and feel my heart beating for you. I've got you my dear, dear little boy.")

_____

_____

_____

3. Now that you have finished with this exercise, read it to a trusted friend. Repeat this exercise for the next five days and see what the Lord brings to your mind.

Restoring My Soul with Others

1. If you feel comfortable, share your experience with the exercise in "Restoring My Soul with God" with your group.

2. What do you think the following verses mean?

   - "Bear one another's burdens, and so fulfill the law of Christ" (Galatians 6:2).
   - "Rejoice with those who rejoice, weep with those who weep" (Romans 12:15).
   - "Blessed are those who mourn, for they shall be comforted" (Matthew 5:4).

3. What are some of the fears or concerns you have about processing hurts from your past? Discuss.

4. What are some reasons why God had the Israelites build altars (see Genesis 35:1; Joshua 4:1-7)?

5. What questions do you have about implicit and explicit memory? How do you see these answers informing your understanding of Christ-formation and the abundant life?

10

THE TRANSFORMING POWER
OF BIBLICALLY INFORMED THINKING

WHEN I WAS TWELVE YEARS OLD and living with my grandparents on our family ranch in southern Utah, there was a door between our bedrooms that gave me a direct line of sight to my grandpa's side of the bed. Every night before falling asleep, I saw him reading his Bible. To be honest, I started to wonder if he was a slow reader because he never seemed to finish that book. But as I became more aware, I realized it wasn't that my grandpa was a slow reader but that he had a deep love for God's Word.

During the three years I lived with my grandparents, my grandpa's love for the Bible rubbed off on me. As a result, during the last forty-three years that I have followed Jesus, I have been deeply committed to reading and studying God's Word. And yet, almost every time I read a familiar passage or story in the Bible today, the Holy Spirit shows me something new. This just reinforces the fact that "the word of God is alive and active" (Hebrews 4:12, NIV). So imagine my surprise—as I continued to study the Bible while writing my doctoral dissertation—to find numerous references in very familiar passages that supported my growing understanding of neuroscience—especially the important role that my thinking played in my own Christ-formation.

In this chapter, I want to share with you my findings from Scripture that support how neuroscience can inform our discipleship to Jesus.

The Biblical Emphasis on Right Thinking

In many of his letters, the apostle Paul refers to the important role Scripture plays in our thought life. For example, in Romans 12:2, Paul commands the believers living in Rome to "be transformed by the renewal of your mind." The Greek word Paul uses for "transformed" is *metamorphoō*, a present, passive imperative. The present tense emphasizes an ongoing, never-ending process of transformation that begins at the moment of salvation, continues throughout our lives, and will be completed in heaven. The passive voice of the verb means that our transformation is not something we can do alone. The power comes from the Holy Spirit, the primary agent behind the process of change (2 Corinthians 3:18). The imperative mood indicates this is not merely a suggestion or a good idea but a command. We obey this command as we study and apply the Scriptures to our lives. As pastor John MacArthur explains in his commentary on Romans, "God's own Word is the instrument His own Holy Spirit uses to renew our minds, which, in turn, He uses to transform our living."[1] Paul's conclusion to Romans 12:2 is this: As we submit ourselves to this work of the Spirit, we are able to discern God's will.

Another example where Paul emphasizes the importance of our thought life is Colossians 3:2: "Set your minds on things above, not on earthly things" (NIV). The Greek word Paul uses for "set your minds" is *phroneō*, which carries the meaning "to have a settled way of understanding, to hold an opinion, and to maintain an attitude."[2] Paul is advocating an outlook of staying focused on the eternal promises and realities that are true for us in Christ.

Jesus is our best example in this. His focus on the realities of heaven gave him strength to endure the agonies of the cross: "Because of the joy awaiting him, he endured the cross, disregarding its shame" (Hebrews 12:2, NLT). We have access to the same mindset as Jesus because we have been given the mind of Christ (1 Corinthians 2:16). The invitation to us is to keep the eyes of our hearts focused on him.[3] Both the apostle Paul and the writer of

Hebrews are exhorting us to view all of life through the lens of Christ; to be present to and live in light of the Father's favor, provision, and protection.

We find another biblical example of Paul emphasizing the importance of right thinking in Philippians 4:8 (noted earlier), where he commands the believers in Philippi to consistently think about "whatever is true, whatever is noble, whatever is right, whatever is pure, whatever is lovely, whatever is admirable—if anything is excellent or praiseworthy—think about such things" (NIV). The expression "think about" is a translation of the Greek word *logizomai*. New Testament scholar Grant Osborne explains its meaning: "to carefully consider and reflect on these qualities, to allow them to permeate our minds and thereby guide our conduct. The present tense stresses the need to dwell continually on these virtues."[4] Biblical thinking is central to both Christ-formation and abundant living. Theologian Robert Saucy wrote, "As we immerse ourselves in God's truth it changes the thinking of our heart and consequently the way we live."[5] Consider the following biblical examples to illustrate the power of thoughts to influence outcomes.

David and Goliath

Saul was the king of Israel, who was at war with the Philistines. Goliath was a giant of a man and a fierce warrior. He was the undefeated Philistine champion who profaned the God of Israel and set a challenge for one Israelite warrior to fight him; the victor would decide the outcome of the war. The Bible says after hearing the words of Goliath, the Israelites were "dismayed and terrified" (1 Samuel 17:11, NIV). Let's take a minute to read between the lines and consider some possible thoughts going through the minds of Saul's warriors.

Maybe some were thinking, *He's so big and strong, no one can defeat him.* Or, *We're going to lose this battle for sure and become slaves to the Philistines.* Or maybe, *All is lost, there is no hope. What are we going to do?* What would you have been thinking about? I probably would have sided with those who thought all was lost.

But that's not what was running through David's mind. After this young shepherd boy—unfamiliar in the ways of war, unskilled with sword and spear, unaccustomed to armor—heard what Goliath said, he was incensed and ready to fight:

David said to the Philistine, "You come to me with a sword and with a spear and with a javelin, but I come to you in the name of the LORD of hosts, the God of the armies of Israel, whom you have defied. This day the LORD will deliver you into my hand, and I will strike you down and cut off your head. And I will give the dead bodies of the host of the Philistines this day to the birds of the air and to the wild beasts of the earth, that all the earth may know that there is a God in Israel, and that all this assembly may know that the LORD saves not with sword and spear. For the battle is the LORD's, and he will give you into our hand."

1 SAMUEL 17:45-47

Instead of letting fear consume his thoughts, David chose to think rightly about both God and Goliath, and the outcome produced a great victory that changed the course of history for himself and the rest of Israel. David's triumph over Goliath was greatly influenced by what he chose to think about. David believed what the Old Testament Scripture reveals is true about God, the one true God, the covenant God of Israel. David believed that Yahweh "determines the number of the stars and calls them each by name. Great is our Lord and mighty in power" (Psalm 147:4-5, NIV). David believed that Yahweh was the one who delivered him from the paws of the lion and the bear when he defended his sheep from attack (1 Samuel 17:37) and that Yahweh would do the same in regard to Goliath. David believed that "The LORD is my strength and my shield; my heart trusts in him, and he helps me" (Psalm 28:7, NIV). David allowed his knowledge of God and his experience with God to inform his thinking, and it changed the outcome of his life forever.

The Spies after Scouting Out the Promised Land

Prior to entering the Promised Land, Moses sent twelve Israelite spies into Canaan to do some reconnaissance. When the spies returned, ten of them were scared to death. We don't need to read between the lines to know what these guys were thinking because we have it recorded in Scripture:

"We can't go up against them! They are stronger than we are!" So they spread this bad report about the land among the Israelites: "The land we traveled through and explored will devour anyone who goes to live there. All the people we saw were huge. We even saw giants there, the descendants of Anak. Next to them we felt like grasshoppers, and that's what they thought, too!"

NUMBERS 13:31-33, NLT

Can't you hear the fear in their voices and see the terror in their eyes as they report back to Moses? Their interpretation of the situation and perspective was totally skewed, and it caused them to be afraid. Their thinking influenced their decision and determined the outcome: We can't take the land.

Joshua and Caleb chose to think about the same situation differently. They saw the same things the other ten spies did, but they chose to look at the situation through an entirely different lens. Instead of being afraid and uncertain, Joshua and Caleb said, "Let us go up at once and occupy it, for we are well able to overcome it" (Numbers 13:30). Because they chose to think differently, Joshua and Caleb experienced different emotions and made different choices, which produced a very different outcome. Of the twelve spies, only Joshua and Caleb were allowed to enter the Promised Land. I would say that their thinking resulted in a very different quality of life.

Elisha, His Servant, and the Aramean Army

Elisha's servant steps outside one morning and discovers that they are surrounded by an army of Arameans, enemies of God's people. Thinking that they were going to be killed, the servant runs back inside and says to Elisha, "Alas, my master! What shall we do?" Elisha responds, saying, "Do not be afraid, for those who are with us are more than those who are with them" (2 Kings 6:15-16). Elisha had eyes to see what his servant could not, and he had a different mindset than his servant because he considered the situation from God's perspective. In order to calm his servant down, Elisha asks the Lord to open his eyes so he can see the truth. The servant looks again and sees "that the hillside around Elisha was filled with horses and chariots of fire" (2 Kings 6:17, NLT).

The Transforming Power of Thinking Biblically

When we choose to think rightly about God and who we are as his sons and daughters, we will experience the challenges of life very differently. Fear is often the result of a distorted perspective brought on by faulty thinking. Instead of allowing lies and distortions of the truth to fill your mind, shift your thoughts to what God says is true. If you train yourself to do that, you will experience a much different outcome.

To think biblically about God is to remember that he is the King of kings, the creator and sustainer of all things through Christ. It is to remember that God is all-powerful, good, loving, compassionate, and kind; he is your heavenly Father who loves you dearly, as much as he loves his only begotten son (John 17:23).

God is always seeking your good. When you think biblically about who God is and who you are to him, you will experience healthy emotions—including love, joy, peace, and hope—that will affect your decisions and produce behavior that is in step with the Spirit (Galatians 5:16-26). And when you choose to think biblically about the truth of who you are in Christ, that you are the son or daughter of God almighty, that you are his beloved, whom he loves with a fierce and tender love, why would you ever choose to dwell on lies and distortions of the truth again? The Holy Spirit uses Scripture to inform our thinking, and as we continue to submit to his work in our lives, we will be transformed.

In the next chapter, we will take a closer look at the person and work of the Holy Spirit in our Christ-formation and how he helps us to experience the abundant life.

Restoring My Soul with God

Biblically informed thoughts directly influence quality of life. This is especially true regarding the thoughts we have toward God. Spend some time reflecting on the Scriptures below and answer the corresponding prompt for each category (presence, provision, and protection):

PRESENCE: God is with me!

- "You keep track of all my sorrows. You have collected all my tears in your bottle. You have recorded each one in your book" (Psalm 56:8, NLT).

- "Be strong. Take courage. Don't be intimidated. Don't give them a second thought because God, your God, is striding ahead of you.

He's right there with you. He won't let you down; he won't leave you" (Deuteronomy 31:6, MSG).

- [The LORD said,] "Yes, be bold and strong! Banish fear and doubt! For remember, the Lord your God is with you wherever you go" (Joshua 1:9, TLB).

- "The LORD your God is living among you. He is a mighty savior. He will take delight in you with gladness. With his love, he will calm all your fears. He will rejoice over you with joyful songs" (Zephaniah 3:17, NLT).

- "You've kept track of my every toss and turn through the sleepless nights, each tear entered in your ledger, each ache written in your book" (Psalm 56:8, MSG).

- "The Word became flesh and dwelt among us, and we have seen his glory, glory as of the only Son from the Father, full of grace and truth" (John 1:14).

- [Jesus said,] "I will ask the Father, and he will give you another Helper, to be with you forever, even the Spirit of truth" (John 14:16-17).

- [Jesus said,] "I am with you always, to the end of the age" (Matthew 28:20).

Ask the Lord to bring to your mind a specific time that he was with you. Describe that situation. Write down why you are grateful to the Lord for his presence. Write out what you think God wants to say to you about that situation.

_____

_____

_____

PROVISION: God will take care of me.

- [Jesus said,] "That is why I tell you not to worry about everyday life—whether you have enough food and drink, or enough clothes to wear.

Isn't life more than food, and your body more than clothing? Look at the birds. They don't plant or harvest or store food in barns, for your heavenly Father feeds them. And aren't you far more valuable to him than they are? Can all your worries add a single moment to your life?

"And why worry about your clothing? Look at the lilies of the field and how they grow. They don't work or make their clothing, yet Solomon in all his glory was not dressed as beautifully as they are. And if God cares so wonderfully for wildflowers that are here today and thrown into the fire tomorrow, he will certainly care for you. Why do you have so little faith?

"So don't worry about these things, saying, 'What will we eat? What will we drink? What will we wear?' These things dominate the thoughts of unbelievers, but your heavenly Father already knows all your needs. Seek the Kingdom of God above all else, and live righteously, and he will give you everything you need.

"So don't worry about tomorrow, for tomorrow will bring its own worries. Today's trouble is enough for today" (Matthew 6:25-34, NLT).

- "My God will supply every need of yours according to his riches in glory in Christ Jesus" (Philippians 4:19).

Ask the Lord to bring to your mind a specific time that He provided for you. Describe that situation. Write down why you are grateful to the Lord for his provision. Write out what you think God wants to say to you about that situation.

_____

_____

_____

PROTECTION: God will protect me.

- [The LORD said,] "Do not be afraid, for I have ransomed you. I have called you by name; you are mine. When you go through deep waters, I will be with you. When you go through rivers of difficulty, you will not drown. When you walk through the fire of oppression, you will not be burned up; the flames will not consume you. For I am the LORD, your God, the Holy One of Israel, your Savior" (Isaiah 43:1-3, NLT).

- "Even when walking through the dark valley of death I will not be afraid, for you are close beside me, guarding, guiding all the way" (Psalm 23:4, TLB).

- "Don't you know anything? Haven't you been listening? GOD doesn't come and go. God *lasts*. He's Creator of all you can see or imagine. He doesn't get tired out, doesn't pause to catch his breath. And he knows *everything*, inside and out. He energizes those who get tired, gives fresh strength to dropouts. For even young people tire and drop out, young folk in their prime stumble and fall. But those who wait upon GOD get fresh strength. They spread their wings and soar like eagles, They run and don't get tired, they walk and don't lag behind" (Isaiah 40:28-31, MSG).

- "The LORD will keep you from all harm—he will watch over your life; the LORD will watch over your coming and going both now and forevermore" (Psalm 121:7-8, NIV).

- [Jesus said,] "My sheep hear my voice, and I know them, and they follow me. I give them eternal life, and they will never perish, and no one will snatch them out of my hand. My Father, who has given them to me, is greater than all, and no one is able to snatch them out of the Father's hand. I and the Father are one" (John 10:27-30).

- "The Lord is faithful, and he will strengthen you and protect you from the evil one" (2 Thessalonians 3:3, NIV).

Ask the Lord to bring to your mind a specific time that he protected you. Describe that situation. Write down why you are grateful to the Lord for his protection. Write down what you think God wants to say to you about that situation.

_____

_____

_____

Restoring My Soul with Others

1. If you feel comfortable, share any insights that came out of your "Restoring My Soul with God" exercises dealing with God's *presence, provision,* and *protection.*

2. How would you define biblically informed thinking?

3. Why is biblically informed thinking important both to Christ-formation and abundant living?

4. Review the biblical examples used in this chapter, and discuss the implications of biblically informed thinking.

5. What is an example (either positive or negative) from your own life that illustrates how thinking influences outcomes?

11

THE ROLE OF THE HOLY SPIRIT
IN CHRIST-FORMATION

FRANCIS CHAN, IN HIS BOOK *FORGOTTEN GOD*, identifies what I believe is a serious problem in the lives of many believers and in the local church (especially evangelical churches) today:

> Having read the Scriptures outside the context of contemporary church culture, you would be convinced that the Holy Spirit is as essential to a believer's existence as air is to staying alive. . . .
>
> There is a big gap between what we read in Scripture about the Holy Spirit and how most believers and churches operate today.[1]

Christ-formation is dependent upon the Holy Spirit as the primary agent for change regarding the dynamics of the heart. In fact, all spiritual/ emotional growth is fundamentally the work of the Holy Spirit. Paul writes, "We all, with unveiled face, beholding the glory of the Lord, are being transformed into the same image from one degree of glory to another. For this comes from the Lord who is the Spirit" (2 Corinthians 3:18). One way the Holy Spirit brings about Christ-formation is through truth: He is the

Spirit of truth and the one who guides believers into all truth (John 16:13). Specific to Christ-formation, the Holy Spirit guides you into the truth about the nature and character of God and all aspects of your identity in Christ. The Holy Spirit will also expose the hurts in your heart that he needs to heal. The Holy Spirit wants to resolve those spiritual/emotional conflicts that are hindering Christ-formation and the greater experience of the abundant life. In this chapter, I will discuss both the person and work of the Holy Spirit specifically as it applies to the process of Christ-formation.

The Holy Spirit Lives in My Heart

The Holy Spirit takes up residence in the heart—the immaterial part of every believer—at the moment of salvation. God promised the indwelling presence of the Holy Spirit in the Old Testament as he spoke through the prophet Ezekiel:

> I will give you a new heart, and a new spirit I will put within you.
> And I will remove the heart of stone from your flesh and give you
> a heart of flesh. And I will put my Spirit within you, and cause
> you to walk in my statutes and be careful to obey my rules.
> EZEKIEL 36:26-27

Jesus told his disciples that the Holy Spirit would come to live in them:

> I will ask the Father and he will give you another Advocate, who
> will never leave you. He is the Holy Spirit, who leads into all truth.
> The world cannot receive him, because it isn't looking for him and
> doesn't recognize him. But you know him, because he lives with
> you now and later will be in you.
> JOHN 14:16-17, NLT

This promise that the Holy Spirit would live in God's people was fulfilled on the day of Pentecost (Acts 2:1-4). Since that day, at the moment of salvation, the Holy Spirit takes up residence in the heart of every believer. Paul writes, "Because you are sons, God has sent the Spirit of his Son into our hearts" (Galatians 4:6).[2] The implications of the indwelling Holy Spirit are all important, but one that we must consider to better understand his role in Christ-formation is that we become a *new creation* in Christ (2 Corinthians 5:17).

Jesus referred to this renewal as being *born again* (John 3:3), and Paul compared it to Jesus' death and resurrection (Romans 6:1-4). One result of this regeneration is that in Christ, every believer has been set free from the power of sin. Paul writes: "We know that our old self was crucified with him in order that the body of sin might be brought to nothing, so that we would no longer be enslaved to sin" (Romans 6:6). The believer is given a new heart with new capacities to live without the encumbrances of sin. Authors Neil T. Anderson and Robert L. Saucy explain,

> Our very being is changed at its deepest level so that we now have new desires and new prevailing dispositions of life. . . . a change in the *fundamental* orientation, propensities, desires, or direction of our person, including our thoughts and actions.[3]

As a result of this renewing work of the Spirit, Paul proclaims, "Therefore, if anyone is in Christ, he is a new creation. The old has passed away; behold, the new has come" (2 Corinthians 5:17). The change that takes place in our hearts at the moment of salvation includes the capacity to think, feel, choose, and act in ways that are godly and life-giving. This all-encompassing change is an act of God's grace accomplished by the power of the Holy Spirit. In other words, as we walk in the Spirit, we are able "to will and to work for his good pleasure" (Philippians 2:13).

This change in the life of the believer is not limited to a new heart but also includes the affirmation of our new identity in Christ.

The Holy Spirit Affirms My Identity in Christ

I once heard TV personality Oprah Winfrey say that "we are all God's children." This is not true. Every person is God's creation, created in his image and likeness, but it is not until a person is born again that he or she becomes a child of God. The apostle John writes, "To all who *did receive* him, who *believed* in his name, *he gave* the right to become children of God, who were born, not of blood nor of the will of the flesh nor of the will of man, but of God" (John 1:12-13, emphasis added). Our new identity as sons and daughters is exclusively the result of God's love for us demonstrated by

Jesus' death on the cross: "See how very much our Father loves us, for he calls us his children, and that is what we are" (1 John 3:1, NLT). In addition to establishing our role in God's own family, the Holy Spirit confirms this truth in our hearts: "The Spirit himself bears witness with our spirit that we are children of God, and if children, then heirs—heirs of God and fellow heirs with Christ" (Romans 8:16-17). Indeed, as God's adopted sons and daughters (Galatians 4:5), we have all the rights and privileges of natural-born children.

It's true that a complete understanding of our familial standing is still a mystery because Scripture doesn't give us a full account of all the details, but what we do have is profound. In Christ, we are Jesus' siblings (Romans 8:29; Hebrews 2:11)[4] and are heirs to all that is his (Romans 8:17). There is more: In Christ, we are now members of a royal priesthood and a holy nation (1 Peter 2:9). Oh, the wonder and scope of our familial standing in Christ is truly beyond what any of us could possibly imagine! Let us never again consider ourselves to be paupers; we are sons and daughters of the King of kings!

How would the quality of your life be different if you lived out the reality of what God says is true about you in Christ? How would you see yourself differently if you chose to look at yourself through God's eyes and believe that what he says about you is true? The fact that you are a son or daughter of God should give you great confidence in his intimate and personal love for you. By choosing to focus your thoughts on what God says is true about you, the Holy Spirit will produce his fruit in your life (Galatians 5:22-23).

The question is this: *Will you replace the perspective you have of yourself that is tainted by lies and distortions of the truth?* The Holy Spirit's renewing work—new life and a new identity—are essential to the Christ-formation process, as they provide the personal evidence of God's love that we need to live securely connected to God.

The Holy Spirit Can Gently Reveal the Wounds in My Heart

Sin wounds the heart. The Psalms are filled with graphic descriptions of the physical and psychological pain that is produced by sin. David experienced physical pain and anguish of heart as a result of his sin of adultery with Bathsheba: "When I kept silent, my bones wasted away through my groaning all day long. For day and night your hand was heavy upon me;

my strength was dried up as by the heat of summer" (Psalm 32:3-4), and in Psalm 38:4-8 (NLT), David laments,

My guilt overwhelms me—
   it is a burden too heavy to bear.
My wounds fester and stink
   because of my foolish sins.
I am bent over and racked with pain.
   All day long I walk around filled with grief.
A raging fever burns within me,
   and my health is broken.
I am exhausted and completely crushed.
   My groans come from an anguished heart.

Jeremiah experienced great anguish of heart in response to God's revelation of coming judgment for the sins of Judah: "My anguish, my anguish! I writhe in pain!" (Jeremiah 4:19). The Bible implies that the heart is a storehouse for emotional pain: "The heart knows its own bitterness" (Proverbs 14:10). Dallas Willard explained that the heart is greatly affected by life experiences:

Our life and how we find the world now and in the future is, almost totally, a simple result of what we have become in the depths of our being—in our spirit, will, or heart. From there we see our world and interpret reality. From there we make our choices, break forth into action, try to change our world. We live from our depths—most of which we do not understand.[5]

Emotional pain does not dissipate by itself over time. Instead, it festers and presents itself in a variety of ways, including distorted thoughts, damaging emotions, and an impaired ability to make good choices. All this works together to promote destructive behavior. Karl Lehman explains how unresolved emotional pain contributes to present problems:

When something in the present activates or "triggers" a traumatic memory, the unresolved toxic content comes out of where it's stored and becomes part of what a person thinks and feels in the present. This coming forward of incompletely processed memory content into the present causes a wide variety of problems, such as addictions, mysterious physical symptoms, post-traumatic stress disorder, anxiety disorders, depression, eating disorders, impaired parenting, difficulty receiving new truth, impaired discernment and blocked peak performance.[6]

Yet, much of the unresolved emotional pain that energize the destructive dynamics of the heart is hidden in its depths and only known by God. Exposing these deeply held hurts in the heart is an important work of the Spirit in Christ-formation.

The sons of Korah reminded the Israelites that God "knows the secrets of the heart" (Psalm 44:21). Ezra revealed that God alone knows the hearts of his people when he prayed, "Forgive, and deal with everyone according to all they do, since you know their hearts (for you alone know the human heart)" (2 Chronicles 6:30, NIV). The Lord spoke through the prophet Jeremiah, saying, "I, GOD, search the heart and examine the mind" (Jeremiah 17:9-10, MSG). When rebuking the Pharisees, Jesus reminded them that "God knows your hearts" (Luke 16:15). While the apostles were trying to discern who should take the place of Judas as the next apostle, they prayed, "You, Lord, who know the hearts of all, show which one of these two you have chosen to take the place in this ministry of apostleship from which Judas turned aside to go to his own place" (Acts 1:24-25). Paul alludes to the fact that only God knows the heart. When speaking to the believers in Thessalonica, Paul says, "We speak, not to please man, but to please God who tests our hearts" (1 Thessalonians 2:4). Finally, in Revelation 2:23, Jesus says, "I am he who searches mind and heart." Biblical evidence indicates that God alone knows the human heart, including all its secret hurts and conflicts.

One way the Holy Spirit helps us to resolve the hurts and conflicts that can hinder Christ-formation is to bring them into our conscious mind to process with God and others. The Holy Spirit exposes what is in our hearts—the painful life experiences and the distorted thoughts we struggle with—because they cannot be properly processed if left in the dark. Jesus said that "the truth will set you free" (John 8:32). The Holy Spirit is "the

Spirit of truth" (John 16:13), the only one who can reveal not only the deep things of God (1 Corinthians 2:10) but also the deep things of the heart.

A good friend is someone who is willing to tell us the truth even if it hurts. The Holy Spirit wants to be this friend. He will not force his way into these secret places and demand we face our hurts and conflicts, but he is ready to respond to our invitation. David models this for us in Psalm 139:23-24: "Search me, O God, and know my heart! Try me and know my thoughts! And see if there be any grievous way in me, and lead me in the way everlasting!" When we ask the Spirit of truth to reveal the hurt or hurtful ways in us, he will do so in a gentle and loving way.

After the Spirit reveals the pain, he will help us process it by rewiring our brains with the knowledge of God. This knowledge includes biblical information about God and our experiences with God.

How the Holy Spirit Can Rewire the Brain

Even though we are a new creation in Christ, God doesn't erase old, painful memories, toxic thoughts, distortions, or faulty interpretations that have been wired into our brains over time. God doesn't just hit the "clear" button at the moment of salvation. Instead, God wants us to process these things in relationship with him and others. Processing promotes greater understanding and maturity.

Earlier I described the trauma I experienced as a little boy after my parents' divorce and during the years I lived in Utah. These experiences wounded my childhood heart and produced a toxic array of feelings which distorted my perspective of God, myself, and others. As I grew older, and after I gave my life to Jesus at age twelve, I did believe that God was my heavenly Father and that he was good, but my toxic emotions remained, hindering my ability to experience God's personal loving care. This array of toxic emotions was triggered once again after I was fired as a senior pastor and came crashing down on me like an avalanche.

I can't recall how many sermons I have preached over the years and how many times I have assured other people—in the midst of difficult times— that God had everything under control, but when I was lying buried under the rubble of my damaged emotions, I struggled greatly with doubt. I didn't doubt God's love and care for others; I doubted in God's love and care for me. There was a conflict raging between what I knew in my head to be true about God—God takes care of his people—and what I felt in my heart was true about God, that God had not taken care of me.

English professor Judith Hougen helped me understand the reason for my conflict in her book *Transformed into Fire*:

> The head can receive a great deal of truth without ever engaging
> the heart because there is a significant difference in how the head
> and the heart come to believe. . . .
> [T]he heart believes only what it experiences. . . . Thus, the
> heart, in order to become convinced of a truth, needs physical
> or psychological experience.[7]

My childhood experiences had given me a limited set of memories to draw from. For most of my adolescence, I felt mostly rejected and alone, and my termination as pastor in adulthood triggered these past emotions. Today, because of my experience with God over the past six years (and a lot of hard inner work), I have closed the gap significantly between my head and my heart.

The toxic emotions and subsequent distorted thoughts I experienced during my childhood trauma did not disappear after I became a Christian, nor were they eliminated by the intellectual knowledge of God that I had gained during seminary and my years as a pastor. I had to work hard to process the pain that resided in the deep places of my heart. And the same is true for you. Resolving the spiritual/emotional conflicts that hinder Christ-formation requires a process that closes the gap between the head and the heart.

According to my experience in ministering to people over the last thirty years, more of us have a greater heart problem than a head problem. In other words, we have an overdeveloped rational understanding of God and an underdeveloped relational experience with God; we need both. Hougen rightly maintains that

> The faith most of us have been handed is almost entirely cognitive,
> a relationship based on the ideas that we form about God or the
> ideas that we direct toward him. We have come to define *belief*
> as only intellectual decision and assent. Love, mercy, grace,

sanctification—all are abstractions rather than living, daily realities, experiences that enflame the soul. If the heart enters into the spiritual equation, it slips in through the back door—usually via the weekend retreat or the mountaintop worship experience.[8]

While we draw a variety of conclusions from all our experiences—positive or negative—the negative experiences usually present the greatest challenge. Research suggests that it is the intensity of an emotion associated with an experience that makes it stick in our memory. When these emotions are negative, they can wire our brains in destructive ways that cause us to resist the love we need to fuel Christ-formation and a greater experience of the abundant life.

So then, how do you remove old unhealthy thoughts and replace them with new healthy thoughts? And how do you build relational experiences with God? What does that process look like? The good news is, it's not as complicated as you might think, and it's not a process you have to do alone. The Holy Spirit, who lives in you, will help you rewire your brain. As you choose to focus your thinking on Scripture, the Holy Spirit will confirm that truth in your heart. And as you practice communing with God, you will begin to experience a greater sense of his presence, peace, and joy.

The Holy Spirit is the agent of Christ-formation and the one who guides us into all truth (John 16:13-14), including the truth about God, self, and others. This means that we can reframe past experiences by replacing lies and distortions with what God says is true.

Please read 1 Corinthians 2:10-16 (NIV) below carefully:

The Spirit searches all things, even the deep things of God. For who knows a person's thoughts except their own spirit within them? In the same way no one knows the thoughts of God except the Spirit of God. What we have received is not the spirit of the world, but the Spirit who is from God, so that we may understand what God has freely given us. This is what we speak, not in words taught us by human wisdom but in words taught by the Spirit, explaining spiritual realities with Spirit-taught words. The person without the Spirit does not accept the things that come from the Spirit of God but considers them foolishness, and cannot understand them because they are discerned only through the Spirit. The person with the Spirit makes judgments about all things, but such a person is not subject to merely human judgments, for,

"Who has known the mind of the Lord
   so as to instruct him?"

But we have the mind of Christ.

Notice that the Holy Spirit knows the deep things of God; these include the thoughts and intentions of his heart. And the Holy Spirit makes God's thoughts and intentions known to us: namely, all that is true about our new life in Christ. As we read and study the Bible, the Spirit will confirm the truth we find in our hearts and bring to our mind the things that God is thinking. We can always test what we hear God saying to us by checking with Scripture: God will never speak to our hearts in a way that is contrary to his Word. The Holy Spirit rewires our brains by confirming God's truth in our hearts.

For example, we read in Scripture that God is love (1 John 4:8), and then the Holy Spirit pours God's love in our hearts as confirmation (Romans 5:5). The Bible declares that God cares for his people: "Do not fear, for I am with you; do not be dismayed, for I am your God. I will strengthen you and help you" (Isaiah 41:10, NIV); and then the Spirit confirms in our heart that God cares for us, too: "Cast all your anxiety on him because he cares for you" (1 Peter 5:7, NIV). Jesus promised that one day he would return to take us to his Father's house (John 14:2-3), and then the Holy Spirit confirms the truth of our heavenly inheritance in our hearts as the "guarantee of our inheritance" (Ephesians 1:14). These are only a few examples of how the Holy Spirit confirms in our hearts the truth we read in the Bible.

In addition to his work of confirmation, the Holy Spirit helps us remember Scripture when we need it. As we focus our attention on the truth in God's Word, especially the words of Jesus, the Holy Spirit brings them to mind. Jesus said, "When you are arrested and stand trial, don't worry in advance about what to say. Just say what God tells you at that time, for it is not you who will be speaking, but the Holy Spirit"

(Mark 13:11, NLT). The more often you choose to think about what God says is true, the more these truths will become patterns of thought. As you think God's thoughts, you will experience healthy emotions that will affect your desires and behavior.

This transformation process in our thinking is primarily the work of the Holy Spirit, but we also get to participate.

How to Partner with the Holy Spirit in Christ-Formation

Distorted thoughts and perceptions form strongholds that can be torn down, but the Holy Spirit does not do this without our participation. This is what Paul refers to in 2 Corinthians 10:5 (NIV): "We demolish arguments and every pretension that sets itself up against the knowledge of God, and we take captive every thought to make it obedient to Christ." The Greek word Paul uses for *arguments* means "thought" or "reasoning." And this demolishing is a continual, ongoing action. The thoughts that are "against the knowledge of God" include lies and distorted perceptions that make up faulty thinking. And when you hold those lies and distorted perceptions up to the light of God's truth—comparing them to what God says is true in Scripture—they are demolished because the truth has exposed the lies. When you replace the lies and distorted perceptions with God's revelation, you will begin to experience more of the abundant life than you ever thought possible. Figure 11.1 illustrates this process.

FIGURE 11.1

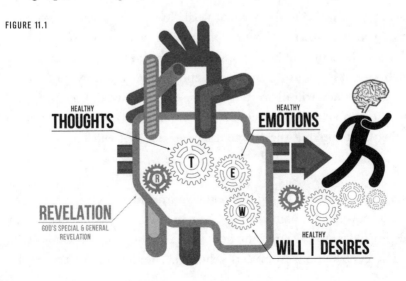

As you focus your thoughts (*attention density* in neuroplasticity) on God's revelation, those neurons wire themselves together more densely, so those thoughts become your default thinking patterns. Over time, as you continue to meditate on God's truth, you automatically lean toward health and life.

But in order for all this to work, you have to walk closely with the Holy Spirit. Three practical ways to do this are to study, meditate on, and memorize Scripture. I don't know of a better way to cultivate a greater capacity to think God's thoughts and partner with the Holy Spirit than to know God's Word. If you never exert the effort it takes to study, meditate on, and memorize Scripture, you will be limited in your capacity to think God's thoughts. In a very literal way, the Holy Spirit rewires your brain the more you internalize God's truth.

All Scripture is helpful in rewiring the brain, but perhaps the most helpful are those verses that teach us the truth about God's love and the various aspects of our new identity in Christ. I agree wholeheartedly with Neil Anderson:

> I believe that your hope for growth, meaning and fulfillment as a
> Christian is based on understanding who you are—specifically, your
> identity in Christ as a child of God. Your understanding of who God
> is and who you are in relationship to Him is the critical foundation
> for your belief system and your behavior patterns as a Christian.[9]

When you choose to think about what God says is true about you "in Christ," you strengthen the neural pathways in your brain that promote qualities of the abundant life. And when you choose to stop thinking toxic thoughts—the lies and distorted perceptions suggested by painful life experiences—they will dissolve over time (Hebb's law and the quantum Zeno effect in action). This emphasis on thinking is very important in rewiring the brain, but there is another exercise that will accentuate the results: Immanuel journaling.

Communing with God Using Immanuel Journaling

I first discovered Immanuel journaling in the book *Joyful Journey* by E. James Wilder, Anna Kang, John Loppnow, and Sungshim Loppnow (with extensive contributions from Karl Lehman). The journal process teaches you how to practice interactive gratitude and attunement with God. I will briefly outline the journaling process below and provide exercises for each at the end of the chapter.

The first Immanuel-journaling exercise is practicing interactive gratitude. This exercise helps to cultivate a greater awareness of God's presence, especially if we are feeling overwhelmed with any of the six big unpleasant emotions identified in *Joyful Journey* as "sadness, anger, fear, shame, hopeless despair, and disgust."[10] This exercise incorporates a time for listening and writing down God's response. You'll find an interactive gratitude exercise you can do at the end of this chapter.

The second Immanuel-journaling exercise takes you through the sequence the brain follows when processing painful memories and emotions. It's a practical way to attune with God. Attunement is a common technique applied by therapists. Karl Lehman says that practicing attunement with God helps people to feel seen, heard, and understood; they feel that God is with them, that God cares for them, and that God is glad to be with them.[11] God attuned to the Israelites in Exodus 3:7-8 through his conversation with Moses:

> Then the LORD said, "I have surely seen the affliction of my
> people who are in Egypt and have heard their cry because of their
> taskmasters. I know their sufferings, and I have come down to
> deliver them out of the hand of the Egyptians and to bring them up
> out of that land to a good and broad land, a land flowing with milk
> and honey."

Notice in this passage how God assures the Israelites he has seen their suffering and heard their cries for help. He spoke of his concern about their situation and committed not only to deliver them from their oppressors but to take them to a Promised Land filled with rich provisions. People can offer attunement to each other, but people are limited. We can experience the benefits of attuning with God all the time. Immanuel journaling offers a structure to do so,

a structure with opportunities to slow down and receive God's validation in the midst of our struggles. When we experience

God's comfort and help we become aware of His presence, and peace is restored to us. . . . Ultimately, Immanuel journaling allows us to become aware of God's good, generous and tender presence in our lives.[12]

Rewiring Is Essential and Biblical

The cognitive aspect for rewiring our brain includes focusing our thoughts on God's revelation. As we take our distortions captive to Christ, we are able to replace lies with truth. The Holy Spirit then confirms this truth in our hearts, rewiring our brain. The relational aspect that rewires the brain cultivates a greater sense of God's presence as we feel cared for and understood.

This rewiring process is essential to both Christ-formation and our capacity to experience the abundant life. In the next chapter, we will dive deeper into the science of love, which will inform our understanding of why relationships are so important to the Christ-formation process.

Restoring My Soul with God
Interactive Gratitude Exercise

Try this exercise for the next five days, writing about five different situations you are grateful for.

1. Pray. Ask the Lord to help you remember something that you are grateful for and write it down in a conversational manner. *Example:* "Lord, thank you for providing for me during the COVID-19 pandemic. I am so grateful to you for your lavish provision for me and my family. As I trust you in this, I feel at peace about the future, knowing that you will provide. Thank you!"

_____

_____

_____

Be present to the feelings of gratitude you are experiencing right now. If you are having difficulty coming up with something, tell the Lord you are struggling and ask him to help you. You'll find that when you share your struggle with God, it takes the pressure off and helps you get unstuck.

2. Reflect on your gratitude statement from above and ask God what he wants to say to you. Write down whatever comes to mind. "Focus on putting down what you sense about His response to your gratitude. This is our humble attempt to hear God."[13] *Example:* "Ken, I love meeting your needs. I have so much more to give you that goes beyond your daily needs. Trust me for your provision and everything else. I am especially fond of you. You are my dear, beloved child. You can rest in confidence that I am with you and will take care of you. Lay yourself down in my green pasture, and be at peace."

_____

_____

_____

Now that you are finished with this exercise, read it to a trusted friend. Reflect on each statement and answer the following question: "Have I worried less this week because of this exercise?"

Attunement Exercise

Set aside forty-five to sixty minutes for this attunement exercise.

1. Begin by reading the story of Hagar in Genesis 16:6-12.

   • Which of the "big six" emotions (sadness, anger, fear, shame, hopeless despair, disgust) do you think Hagar was feeling?

_____

_____

_____

2. Ask the Holy Spirit to help you remember a time when you felt one or more of the "big six" emotions. Write down your experience using

the following questions: *What happened? Where did it happen? Who was present?* and *How old were you?*

_____

_____

_____

3. Now that you remember that painful experience and you are present to your emotions, write about your observable actions and surroundings as if God is describing them back to you. *Example:* "Ken, I see you sitting at your desk with your head in your hands." "I can see your cup of coffee and that you are sitting in the room alone."

_____

_____

_____

4. From God's perspective, write about your body movements, sensations, expressions, or responses that someone else might not notice if they were sitting with you. *Example:* "Ken, I can see that your shoulders are tense." "I can see that your heart is racing." "I can see that you are feeling very sad." "I can see the tears welling up in your eyes." "I can see that you are having trouble remembering anything that is good." "I can see the butterflies in your stomach."

_____

_____

_____

5. Now move into a stage called "God Hears You." Write out what God is hearing you say and what you are thinking. Listen to what God describes to you, and notice how carefully he is paying attention to

what you are saying and thinking. *Example:* "Ken, I can hear you crying." "I can hear you yelling." "I know you're thinking: *God doesn't love me. God won't forgive me for my anger, my bitterness, my jealousy. I don't trust you, God. I feel afraid and uncertain about this situation. I just want all this pain to go away.*"

_____

_____

_____

6. Continue writing down the unspoken words in your mind. God already knows your thoughts; he is not going to strike you down or judge you. He wants you to identify them and share them with him. It's okay; you can be honest. *Examples:* "Ken, I hear you judging yourself." "I know your mind is racing." "I know you're afraid to be honest about your feelings." "I hear you thinking you don't deserve my love." "I hear you saying to yourself, *I should be angry. It's not fair. She can't do this to me. I don't deserve this. After everything I've done for them. I should have known; I'm so stupid.*" "Ken, I hear the fears that you are too ashamed to acknowledge."

_____

_____

_____

7. Now begins the stage called "God Understands." Many times, we judge the things that make us sad by comparing our problems with greater problems of others. But God doesn't do that. God cares about what is bothering you, and he understands. Write down what God is saying to you that validates your pain. *Examples:* "Ken, I can see this is a big deal for you, and I'm sorry." "You feel like you are drowning, don't you?" "This is as big as your parents' divorce." "This is a big deal, but I'm bigger. I can help you." "I understand how sad you feel about this." "I understand how angry and hurt you feel." "I know your heart is filled with fear, but I am here." "I know

how impatient your stepfather was with you and how you got on his nerves, but I am not him."

_____

_____

_____

8. Next comes the stage called "God Is Glad to Be with You." Sometimes we think there is a big pile of sin between us and God. It's easy to think that God loves us more when we do good than when we sin, that our weaknesses disappoint God. But God knows everything we will ever do, so how can he be disappointed? God loves each of us as much in this moment as he will ever love us. Read the story about Peter's betrayal of Jesus (Luke 22:54-62) and then how Jesus restored him (John 21:15-17). Jesus loved Peter in spite of his sin. Write down God's confirmation of his love for you. *Examples:* "I am so glad to see you, Ken; I love hanging out with you." "I am so proud of you." "I am always interested in how you feel and what you are thinking." "You are my beloved child." "I am glad and thankful that you are here with me, that you are listening to me tell you how much you matter to me."

_____

_____

_____

9. The final step is called "God Can Do Something about What You Are Going Through." Review the story of Hagar (Genesis 16:6-12). How did God show her his goodness? How did God promise to help her even though he wasn't going to change her immediate situation?

_____

_____

_____

10. Write down your impressions of what you think God wants to do for you. *Examples*: "Ken, I will be with you no matter what. I want to walk through the pain with you. How can you know I'm your provider if you are never in need? How can you know I'm your comforter if you never feel sad or alone? Your circumstances do not need to change for you to experience my joy and peace." "I will give you strength." "Do not forget that this life is not all there is; there is so much more. Keep one eye on eternity." "I want you to know that I am working behind the scenes of your situation, doing things that you are not aware of. Trust in me."

_____

_____

_____

Restoring My Soul with Others

1. If you feel comfortable, share your experience with the interactive gratitude or attunement exercises.

2. How would you explain our part in the Christ-formation process? How would you explain the role of the Holy Spirit?

3. How do you understand the difference between the head and the heart? Have you ever experienced a gap between the two?

4. Review the "Identity in Christ" list (Appendix C). Which of these aspects is the Holy Spirit confirming for you today? What does that mean to you?

5. Review Figure 11.1 on page 123. How would you describe the impact of God's revelation on the heart?

12

THE TRANSFORMING POWER
OF GOD'S LOVE

GOD IS A RELATIONAL BEING WHO has existed in the loving community of Father, Son, and Holy Spirit for all eternity. God created you in his image and likeness (Genesis 1:27), which means you are a relational being too, created to live in loving community with God and other people. Because God is relational, the Christ-formation process is also relational. You cannot transform into the image of Christ—nor can you experience the abundant life that is available to you—by yourself.

This emphasis on the human need for relationships goes all the way back to the Garden of Eden. In the account of creation, the only thing that God said was *not* good was man being alone (Genesis 2:18). It is a well-established fact, both biblical and scientific: Relationships promote life; isolation promotes death. Anthropologists have discovered that regardless of exercise or diet, people who belong to a loving community experience less cancer and heart disease than those who live alone.[1] All life on planet Earth requires relationships in order to thrive. This is true even for rodents.

Rat Park

In the late 1970s, Canadian psychologist Bruce Alexander and his colleagues at Simon Fraser University in British Columbia conducted a study on drug addiction using rats as the subjects. One group of rats was placed alone in a small cage with a device that enabled the rats to ingest small doses of heroin, morphine, amphetamines, cocaine, and other drugs by pushing on a lever. Under normal conditions—that is, without any precipitating shocks or other stress-inducing factors—these isolated rats consumed large quantities of the available drugs and became addicted. The results of this first test seemed to prove that once a rat ingested drugs, consuming more was simply irresistible.

Alexander and his colleagues were not convinced, however. They realized that rats were highly social creatures, so placing them in solitary confinement wasn't an accurate predictor of their behavior. Alexander writes,

> Solitary confinement drives people crazy; if prisoners in solitary have the chance to take mind-numbing drugs, they do. Might isolated rats not need to numb their minds in solitary confinement for the same reason that people do?[2]

Alexander and his team built a large plywood box on the floor in their laboratory and created what can only be described as a rat utopia. They filled the box with wood chips, different-sized boxes and empty cans to explore, wheels to run on, plenty of food and water, and most importantly, a large community of friendly rats. The experiment was called Rat Park.

The scientists discovered that when the Rat Park rodents were given the same opportunity to ingest drugs as the rats in the solitary-confinement group, after tasting the drug, they chose to avoid it. Even more striking was the fact that when they placed the drug-addicted rats who had formerly been in solitary confinement in the Rat Park community, they lost all interest in the drugs, even subjecting themselves to voluntary detox that caused them to shake uncontrollably.

When given the opportunity, rats preferred relationships over drugs. Experiments like Rat Park point to the power of communal living. Relationships promote a quality of life that cannot be experienced in isolation. In fact, research indicates that prolonged periods of loneliness contribute to poor health and, in some cases, can lead to death.

Loneliness and Death

In 1977, James Lynch made an important contribution to the science of love by studying cardiac-death statistics for nonmarried people. Lynch writes,

> The mortality statistics for heart disease among those adult Americans who are not married are striking—the death rate from heart disease is as much as two to five times higher for nonmarried individuals, including those who are divorced, widowed, or single, than for married Americans.[3]

Lynch is not alone in his findings that people need loving connection with others. Professor Anthony Walsh of Boise State University argues, "Love is not merely theologically or philosophically desirable but is also a biological and psychological necessity."[4] Anthropologist Ashley Montagu pointed out the importance of human relationships when he wrote, "Without love there can be no healthy growth or development, no real life."[5]

Another important discovery in the area of the human need for relationships was made in the 1930s by psychiatrist John Bowlby, who developed a theory on the topic. His attachment theory is defined as the "lasting psychological connectedness between human beings."[6]

Attachment Theory

Bowlby worked at a child-guidance clinic in London, where he treated children who had emotional disabilities. His research revealed that "major disruptions in the mother-child relationship promote later psychopathology." In other words, "children experienced intense distress when separated from their mothers, even if they were fed and cared for by others."[7]

Scientists have also discovered a system in the brain that reveals the need for human connection. Neuroscientist Amir Levine and psychologist Rachel Heller explain,

> The need to be near someone special is so important that the brain has a biological mechanism specifically responsible for creating and regulating our connection with our attachment figures (parents, children, and romantic partners). The mechanism, called the

attachment system, consists of emotions and behaviors that ensure that we remain safe and protected by staying close to our loved ones.[8]

One extreme example that demonstrates the importance of relational connection was a group of experiments conducted by Harry Harlow and Stephen Suomi using rhesus monkeys. Today, these experiments would be considered cruel and unusual; however, these experiments did provide important findings that challenged the way parents were raising their children at the time. Behaviorism—promoted by John B. Watson and B. F. Skinner—maintained that children did not require affection in order to thrive but only needed the necessities: water, food, clothing, and shelter. Thankfully, Harlow and Suomi's monkey experiments turned the theory of behaviorism upside down.

In one experiment, Harlow and Suomi placed newborn baby rhesus monkeys in isolation chambers for three-, six-, nine-, and twelve-month periods of time. During their isolation, the monkeys were observed clutching themselves, sitting catatonic in a corner, and rocking back and forth. When these monkeys were finally released into general population with other monkeys, they were fearful and exhibited hostile behavior toward the other primates. The isolated monkeys also exhibited self-mutilating behavior: tearing out hair, scratching and biting their own arms and legs. The monkeys isolated for three months were the least socially affected long term, but those in isolation for twelve months or longer never recovered. Harlow and Suomi concluded that "total social isolation for at least the first 6 months of life enormously damages or destroys subsequent . . . behavioral capabilities."[9]

Relationships are central to life. General revelation displays that God placed the need for relationships in the DNA of all living creatures. The love that is shared in relationships is required for life. You could say that love is the essential ingredient for all growth.

The brain safeguards the set of beliefs that form our identity in two ways. First, this system operates faster than conscious thought; second, it can only be formed or changed in relationships where we have formed attachment love. This is why beliefs about identity are particularly resistant—they are protected by a shield that requires attachment love before entry.

God's Love Energizes Christ-Formation

John Lennon was at least partly right when he sang, "All you need is love."[10] Love is the most powerful force in this world, but to grow and thrive, a particular kind of love is needed. Christ-formation is largely dependent on God's love—unique because it is unconditional, is always available, and is focused on the best interests of another.

The Greeks defined love using four different words. *Storgē* referred to love for family. *Eros* referred to erotic love. *Philia* referred to brotherly love (specifically, the love you would have for a friend). *Agapē* was the Greek word most commonly used to refer to God's love. Throughout the New Testament, the word used to describe God's love is *agapē*. Paul's famous love passage describes it like this:

> Love [agapē] is patient and kind; love [agapē] does not envy or
> boast; it is not arrogant or rude. It does not insist on its own way;
> it is not irritable or resentful; it does not rejoice at wrongdoing, but
> rejoices with the truth. Love [agapē] bears all things, believes all
> things, hopes all things, endures all things.
>
> Love [agapē] never ends.
>
> 1 CORINTHIANS 13:4-8

Agapē refers to who God is, not just to what he does. John writes that "God is love [agapē]" (1 John 4:8). Therefore, agapē is an expression of God's nature and the motive behind everything he does. The simple fact is this: God loves people because it is his nature to love.

God distributes agapē as a gift to be received; it cannot be earned in any way. In order to receive it, I must believe that God loves me for *who I am* in Christ, not *what I do* for Christ. I must make myself both humble (acknowledging that I am not self-sufficient, that I need God's love) and vulnerable (opening myself to God's love, letting it flow into my heart).

The vulnerability required to receive God's love is especially difficult because it activates the fear of being hurt. Even though fear of being hurt by God is a distortion of the truth, it is often a lie we choose to believe because of the shame we feel as a result of sin.

Conditional versus Unconditional Love

Toxic shame promotes feelings of being unworthy of God's love. This is true, but not the point. It is impossible to be deserving of God's love in any way. God loves you simply and only because he chooses to love you; there is no other "good" reason. Human worth is decreed by God and given unconditionally.

This is a difficult concept for us to grasp, because everywhere we turn, our value is based on our performance. I once attended a professional basketball game where Michael Jordan was playing. It was amazing to me that after missing a few jump shots, the adulation of the crowd changed from excitement to disappointment. Even at the height of his career, Michael Jordan was only as good as his last bucket.

I remember when I was preaching every weekend and felt like I was only as good as my last sermon. I pictured people sitting in the seats holding up score cards to tell me how I was doing. To be honest, I don't remember seeing a lot of 10s. It seems like everything we do is evaluated by our performance. If we do well on an exam, we get an *A*; if we run fast, we win the race; if we are funny, people tend to like us; if we are attractive, we draw people's attention. Performance is so consistently reinforced in our world that thinking of being loved by God regardless of how we perform seems unnatural.

That's why legalism and moralism are so popular in relation to God. Legalism is a sense of merited favor based on obedience to God's commands; moralism is an attempt to earn God's love by being good. Both are subtle attempts to be in control. The thought is, *If I obey God, then he has to bless me*, or *If I am good, then God has to love me*. Many people hold these beliefs without even realizing it. Just pay attention the next time you ask someone the question, "How are you doing?" If they are doing well, they will most likely say something like the following: "Oh man, I'm too blessed to be stressed. My job is good, my marriage is strong, my kids are doing well in school, Johnny caught the game-winning touchdown at homecoming, and Sally got the lead in her school play." Do you hear it? The subtle belief here is that the sign of God's blessing is when things are going well.

It is so easy to fall into the trap and think, *If I do this, then God will do that.* We might not think it directly, but this understanding is implied: *If I'm a good boy or girl, then God will love me.* But agapē is unconditional. Agapē is not a prize for performance.

To be loved without conditions is foreign to our human experience. Every act of human love has some string—however thin and seemingly indiscernible—attached. It's just a part of living in a quid-pro-quo world: Everything is given with the expectation of some kind of a return. There is no worldly equivalent for agapē to help us understand it fully: It is truly supernatural.

And yet, God created the human heart to run on agapē like a high-performance automobile runs on high-octane gasoline. Without agapē, believers cannot mature into their full potential in Christ, nor can they experience the abundant life that he has made available. Without agapē, you can only survive—you can never thrive.

God delivers agapē through two primary relational sources: *divine* and *human*. One aspect of the Holy Spirit's work is to help you internalize God's agapē. Paul writes, "God's love [agapē] has been poured into our hearts through the Holy Spirit who has been given to us" (Romans 5:5). This confirming work of the Spirit includes the subjective, emotional sense of being loved by God.[11] As you choose to believe in God's agapē, you will experience its transforming effects. The assurance of God's agapē creates a secure attachment with God and a safe place to expose and process painful memories.

Jesus likened this connection using the metaphor of a vine and its branches. Jesus said, "I am the vine; you are the branches. Whoever abides in me and I in him, he it is that bears much fruit" (John 15:5). New Testament scholar D. A. Carson maintains that the nature of this fruit includes "obedience to Jesus' commands . . . experience of Jesus' joy . . . love for one another . . . and witness to the world."[12] It is through this abiding relationship with Jesus that the Holy Spirit pours the agapē of God into our hearts, which we are then commanded to share with each other: "We love [agapaō] because he first loved [agapaō] us" (1 John 4:19).

Therefore, believers who make up the body of Christ in this world become the conduits through which the agapē of God flows into the world. But what does it look like to love others with God's agapē? Let me explain how I understand this using the illustration of a waterfall.

Imagine you're standing under a gushing waterfall and the water flowing over you is the agapē of God. Some of the water will splash onto others who are standing close by. Your agapē for others comes out of the overflow of God's agapē for you. Therefore, the more you internalize God's agapē, the more it can flow over you and onto others. Essentially, you become a physical means through which the waters of agapē flow.

This is how we obey the commands to love one another in the New Testament. Almost all of these commands use a form of the word *agapē*. Consider the following examples (emphasis mine):

- "A new commandment I give to you, that you *love* [agapaō] one another: just as I have *loved* [agapaō] you, you also are to *love* [agapaō] one another" (John 13:34-35).

- "Owe no one anything, except to *love* [agapaō] each other" (Romans 13:8).

- "*Love* [agapaō] one another earnestly from a pure heart" (1 Peter 1:22).

- "We should *love* [agapaō] one another" (1 John 3:11).

- "This is his commandment, that we believe in the name of his Son Jesus Christ and *love* [agapaō] one another, just as he has commanded us" (1 John 3:23).

- "Beloved, let us *love* [agapaō] one another, for *love* [agapē] is from God, and whoever *loves* [agapaō] has been born of God and knows God" (1 John 4:7).

- "Beloved, if God so *loved* [agapaō] us, we also ought to *love* [agapaō] one another. No one has ever seen God; if we *love* [agapaō] one another, God abides in us and his *love* [agapē] is perfected in us" (1 John 4:11-12).

- "I am writing to remind you, dear friends, that we should *love* [agapaō] one another" (2 John 1:5, NLT).

I can't overstate how important it is for our own Christ-formation to internalize the agapē of our heavenly Father through our abiding relationship with Jesus Christ and the confirmation of the Holy Spirit, through which the agapē of God flows. Even Jesus needed to experience the Father's agapē through the confirmation of the Spirit and his friends. If Jesus needed agapē, how much more do we?

Jesus Was Aware of the Father's Agapē

The first thing Jesus heard after coming out of the water of his baptism was the Father saying, "This is my dearly loved [agapētos] Son, who brings me great joy" (Matthew 3:17, NLT). Even before Jesus did anything in the way of formal ministry, the Father affirmed him with his unconditional agapē. Jesus made numerous references to his Father's love. In John 3:35, Jesus said, "The Father loves [agapaō] the Son and has given all things into his hand." While standing on the Mount of Transfiguration, Jesus—along with Peter, James, and John—heard the Father say, "This is my beloved [agapētos] Son, with whom I am well pleased; listen to him" (Matthew 17:5). Peter references this momentous occasion on the Mount of Transfiguration:

> When he received honor and glory from God the Father, and the voice was borne to him by the Majestic Glory, "This is my beloved [agapētos] Son, with whom I am well pleased," we ourselves heard this very voice borne from heaven, for we were with him on the holy mountain.
>
> 2 PETER 1:17-18

Again, Jesus said to his disciples in John 15:9, "As the Father has loved [agapaō] me, so have I loved [agapaō] you." Jesus' awareness of the Father's agapē contributed to his quality of life.

The Transforming Power of Unconditional Love

When you know you are loved—I mean really believe in the core of your being that you belong, that you are wanted, and that you are accepted unconditionally no matter what you've done in the past, no matter what you're struggling with in the present, and no matter what you could ever do in the future—you will begin to experience a very different quality of life. God's agapē is the most powerful, life-changing force in the universe.

During the many years I was a local church pastor, I delivered dozens of sermons and used countless illustrations to confirm God's love for the people I served. In addition, I have read the Bible cover to cover many times, I have memorized numerous verses about God's love, and I even know many of the intricate details of God's love imbedded in the original languages in the Bible. But when I was terminated from my job as senior pastor, I went into a tailspin of doubt and confusion. *Does God really love me? Is God going to provide for me?* Today it's evident to me that much of what I knew about God's love in my head had not made its way down to my heart. I could bolster others' confidence in God's everlasting agapē, constant presence, and unlimited resources to endure all things, but sadly, in the wake of my termination, I wondered if everything I had taught and believed that God could do for others would also be done for me.

A few weeks after my termination, I sat poolside with my wife at a local resort where both of our daughters worked. Because of their employment, we enjoyed the luxurious facilities free of charge. So one afternoon, my wife and I decided to take the day off to read and process by the pool at the Montage, overlooking the ocean. Even though the setting could not have been more beautiful and relaxing, I felt anxious and depressed. I certainly wasn't experiencing God's boundless agapē. Instead, I felt like I was drowning in a pool filled with shame and fear. And yet, God was there—as he always is—and he was preparing to remind me of his love in a very dramatic way.

I looked up into the sky and saw the beginning letters of a skywriting message being formed by an airplane. The first letter was "I," followed by "L-O-V-E," and then "Y-O-U." As the pilot prepared to finish the last word, I thought, *Oh, that's nice; some guy is showing his girlfriend or wife how much he loves her by having it written in the sky.* But the plane kept skywriting: first a "K," followed by an "E," and then—yep, you guessed it—an "N." The complete phrase read, "I L-O-V-E Y-O-U K-E-N." I was so startled that I asked my wife to look up to make sure she saw it too.

I don't know who the Ken guy was, or who the message was from, but as far as I'm concerned, God was telling me how much he loved me by writing it in the sky! Today, when I have moments of doubt about God's agapē for me, I think back to that day. I will never forget that moment.

Maybe God has never written a message in the sky for you, at least as far as you know. But God is constantly revealing his love and presence to us; we just need to pay more attention.

Experiencing God's Love through My Senses

God created us with sight, smell, taste, touch, and hearing. Each of these five senses[13] are designed by God to transmit certain information to our brain. For example, Jesus invited Thomas to touch his wounds to stimulate his faith (John 20:27). Human touch releases the hormone oxytocin, which stimulates the feeling of being loved and cared for. "Physical touch increases levels of dopamine and serotonin, two neurotransmitters that help regulate mood and relieve stress and anxiety."[14] In fact, you could say that Jesus' ministry was one of touch. In Mark's Gospel alone, we find six examples: Jesus healed Peter's mother-in-law as he took her hand and helped her up (Mark 1:31). Jesus healed the leper with a touch (Mark 1:41-42). Jesus raised a girl from the dead after taking her by the hand (Mark 5:41-42). Jesus healed the deaf man who could barely speak by putting his fingers in his ears and touching his tongue (Mark 7:33-35). Jesus healed a blind man with his touch in Mark 8:22-26. After casting a demon out of a boy, "Jesus took him by the hand and lifted him to his feet" (Mark 9:27, NIV). Jesus knew the human need to be touched and the powerful results that follow.

In Romans 1:20, Paul reminds us that we experience qualities of God's divine nature through creation. David said, "Oh, taste and see that the LORD is good!" (Psalm 34:8). Moses saw the angel of the Lord in flames of fire from a burning bush (Exodus 3:2), and David saw the glory of God as he looked to the sky (Psalm 19:1). God is ever present, and we see his fingerprints all over creation.

I experience God's loving presence during a sunset, when I look into the night sky at my friend's Montana ranch and see the Milky Way, or when I look into the eyes of my beautiful wife, whom God gave to me thirty-four years ago. I hear God's love in the chirping of a bird as I sit in my backyard, or as the waves crash on the beach, or through the sounds of a rushing river or the wind blowing through the trees. I smell God's love as I cut the roses in my garden or breathe in the smell of salt air at the beach. I taste God's love when I eat vanilla ice cream or my favorite carrot cake baked by our dear friend. I touch God's love when I plant flowers or work on a carpentry project. In all these things, I am interacting with God's creation, paying attention to his glory in all that he has made.

This might sound a bit sentimental, but I think it's a practical way to put Philippians 4:8 into practice: "Fix your thoughts on what is true, and honorable, and right, and pure, and lovely, and admirable. Think about things that are excellent and worthy of praise" (NLT). I want to consecrate these emotionally resonant experiences so that my brain associates them with the loving care and presence of God. What would it look like for you to do the same? How do *you* experience God's love and presence through your senses? In a very real way, our senses become portals through which the Holy Spirit can pour God's agapē into our hearts.

My wife and I have spent a lot of time meditating on Ephesians 3:14-19. We have both committed it to memory, and I review it often throughout the day:

> For this reason I bow my knees before the Father, from whom every family in heaven and on earth is named, that according to the riches of his glory he may grant you to be strengthened with power through his Spirit in your inner being, so that Christ may dwell in your hearts through faith—that you, being rooted and grounded in love, may have strength to comprehend with all the saints what is the breadth and length and height and depth, and to know the love of Christ that surpasses knowledge, that you may be filled with all the fullness of God.

I am especially drawn to the words "to know the love of Christ that surpasses knowledge." The Greek word Paul uses for "know" is *ginōskō*, which refers to both a cognitive and an experiential knowledge of God through our senses.[15] You can know all about the linguistic nuances of God's love in Scripture, you can even memorize every verse that refers to God's love, but if you don't experience it, through your senses or in your relationships with other believers, you will struggle to know God's love and experience his presence in a personal and intimate way.

In order for God's love to make a transforming difference in your life, you need both facts and feelings. For example, it is a fact that God the Father loves you in the same way and to the same degree that he loves Jesus, his Son. Please read that sentence again. Let it soak into the deep places of your heart. What feelings does it evoke for you? Will you believe it, that

God loves you as much as he loves Jesus? It's a truth that will deeply impact your quality of life.

Does God Really Love Me?

When Jesus was praying for his disciples in John 17, he stated clearly that the Father loves every believer in the same way and to the same degree that he loves the Son: "I in them and you in me, that they may become perfectly one, so that the world may know that you sent me and loved them *even as you loved me*. . . . I made known to them your name, and I will continue to make it known, that the love with which you have loved me may be in them, and I in them" (John 17:23, 26, emphasis added). As you read those words, I want you to hear Jesus saying to you, "My Father loves [insert your name] as much as he loves me." That statement should absolutely blow you away!

Two New Testament scholars whom I greatly respect, Craig Keener and D. A. Carson, seem to be blown away by Jesus' words here in John 17 too. Keener (we read this earlier) writes, "That the Father loved Jesus' disciples 'even as' he loved Jesus is one of the most remarkable statements of the Gospel, given the enormity of God's love for his uniquely obedient Son."[16] D. A. Carson agrees:

> The thought is breathtakingly extravagant. . . . that Christians themselves have been caught up into the love of the Father for the Son, secure and content and fulfilled because loved by the Almighty himself, with the *very same love* he reserves for his Son.[17]

These two scholars know the Bible inside and out, and they are blown away by the extravagant love of God.

There is even more evidence of the Father's love for you than this. God's agapē is both constant and consistent. In other words, God's love for you never changes; he loves you as much in this moment as he will ever love you. No matter what you do as a believer, nothing can separate you from the love of God in Christ. Paul writes,

> I am convinced that nothing can ever separate us from God's love. Neither death nor life, neither angels nor demons, neither our fears for today nor our worries about tomorrow—not even the powers

of hell can separate us from God's love. No power in the sky above or in the earth below—indeed, nothing in all creation will ever be able to separate us from the love of God that is revealed in Christ Jesus our Lord.

ROMANS 8:38-39, NLT

I am struck by how emphatic Paul is about God's love for us. And yet, my experience is that in spite of these unequivocal biblical statements, God's love is still abstract for many people. Is that true for you? Is it difficult for you to experience how much God really loves you? If it is, I want you to know that at times it is so for many believers, even for someone as renowned as Dwight L. Moody.

D. L. Moody is considered by many to be one of the greatest evangelists of the nineteenth century. One Sunday in 1868, Moody asked a man named Henry Moorhouse to preach in his place while he was away on a trip. Moorhouse had a dramatic conversion to Christ in 1861 after hearing the story of the Prodigal Son. Those who knew Moorhouse before his conversion said that he had a history of drinking, gambling, and a violent temper and that he carried a gun not to defend himself but to end his own life at some point because he was so unhappy.[18]

After Moorhouse heard about the Father's love for the Prodigal Son, he was convinced that God could love him, too. This deep conviction of God's love compelled him to preach on it whenever he had the opportunity, as he did that day at Moody's church.

When Moody returned home the following week, he asked his wife, Emma, how she liked Moorhouse's sermon. She replied, "I liked it very much, but he preaches a little differently than you do."

"How is that?" Moody inquired.

Emma replied, "He tells the worst sinners that God loves them."

Moody quickly responded, "Well then, he is wrong."

The following Sunday, Moody asked Moorhouse to preach again so he could hear for himself what Moorhouse had to say about God's love. Biographer John Pollock wrote about Moody's reaction:

Moorhouse announced his text: "John 3:16: God so loved the world, that He gave His only begotten Son, that whosoever believeth in

Him should not perish, but have everlasting life." Instead of dividing the text into firstly, secondly, thirdly in ministerial manner, Moorhouse, Moody noted, "went from Genesis to Revelation giving proof that God loves the sinner, and before he got through, two or three of my sermons were spoiled." Moody's teaching that it was the sinner God hates, the sinner as well as the sin, lay shattered at his feet. "I never knew up to that time that God loves us so much. This heart of mine began to thaw out: I could not keep back the tears."[19]

If you have ever doubted that God's love for you is constant and consistent, you're not alone. But like Moody, you have the opportunity to discard the lies you believe about God's love and embrace the truth, the truth that God loves you with the same love that he has for Jesus Christ, his Son. And the more you choose to live out of the reality of God's agapē for you, the more you will experience the abundant life that Jesus has made available.

Agapē energizes the Christ-formation process and makes a greater experience of the abundant life possible. But what exactly is God's love, and how does it differ from human love?

The Nature of God's Love

You can survive on human love, but you can only thrive on God's love, because agapē and human love are two very different things.

Imagine God's love like various grades of gasoline. When you fill up your car at the gas station, you usually have three grades of unleaded fuel available at the pump. Each grade contains a different percentage of octane. For example, regular unleaded gas is rated at 87 octane, midgrade unleaded gas has 89 octane, and premium unleaded gas has an octane level between 91 and 93. All three types of gasoline will work in your car, but if you drive a new car or a sports car with a high-performance engine, you should use higher-octane fuel so that your car will run at maximum capacity. If you use a lower-octane fuel in a high-performance engine, you will hear a knocking sound in the engine when you accelerate. This knocking is the result of gas burning out of synch with your engine's timing. If allowed to persist, this can damage the engine.

Similarly to different grades of fuel, God's love and human love produce different results. God created the human heart to run on his love, high-octane agapē. And one way to experience the agapē of God is through relationships with the people of God, in the body of Christ.

Relationships with other believers who give us safe feedback can help us resolve the spiritual/emotional conflicts that hinder Christ-formation. Believers are uniquely able—through the indwelling presence and power of the Holy Spirit—to be ambassadors of Christ (2 Corinthians 5:20) and conduits of God's love (John 13:35). "Safe" feedback facilitates attunement—the feelings of being seen, heard, understood, and cared for. You know you have received safe feedback when you feel less fearful and alone and more secure and confident.

I have seen firsthand how healing safe feedback can be. After I gave a message at a men's retreat about the spiritual/emotional growth that often follows when we share our pain with others, something incredible happened to a man named Kevin.

Kevin was a senior corpsman in the United States Navy, part of the first group to enter Iraq during the Iraq War in 2003. Kevin and his battalion were engaged in heavy combat for days on end, resulting in many casualties. At one point during the war, Kevin and his medical team were given an assignment to exhume shallow graves in search of Americans. As the senior NCO, Kevin didn't want to expose his men to this horrific task, so he did the work alone. The task traumatized Kevin to the extent that he lost his ability to taste and smell. This condition continued for years—until he attended the men's retreat.

The men at the retreat were ambassadors of Christ to Kevin, providing a safe place to be real about his traumatic experiences without fear of being judged, criticized, rejected, or abandoned. And the results were amazing. While he was walking through the woods—having some alone time with God—suddenly, he could smell the pine trees. Then at dinner, he was able to taste his food. It was a miracle! Later that evening, Kevin shared his story with the men, and we rejoiced together for what God had done. There wasn't a dry eye in the place.

Since then, Kevin and I have become good friends. I can assure you his sense of smell and taste are fully functioning.

Kevin's story reminds me of Paul's words: "Carry each other's burdens, and in this way you will fulfill the law of Christ" (Galatians 6:2, NIV). The law of Christ is to love each other as Jesus has loved us: sacrificially and unconditionally. One way to show this love is to make time to listen to others' painful stories and provide safe feedback.

Something powerful happens to our thought process when we share our stories of pain with people who give us safe feedback. Psychiatrist Curt Thompson explains,

> You construct your understanding of the world and your place in it through the lens of your own story. And the manner and context in which you reflect on your story (in your mind) or tell your story (to others) become part of the fabric of the narrative itself. In other words, the process of reflecting on and telling others your story, and the way you experience others hearing it, actually shapes the story *and the very neural correlates, or networks, it represents.*[21]

When we share our painful stories with others, the safe feedback they give us can actually change how we understand those experiences. If the person responds with empathy, compassion, and acceptance, we feel loved and the shame and distorted thinking associated with it begins to dissipate. Shame is perpetuated by secrecy, but once we share it with others who give us safe feedback, a healing process ensues, mitigating the shame and promoting new understanding. This is what happened with Kevin. After receiving safe feedback from me and the other men at the retreat, he was free to embrace a new understanding of his traumatic experience and thereby a new perspective that promoted a very different quality of life.

Kevin's story is not an isolated event. Over the last thirty years as a pastor, I have had the privilege to give safe feedback to many people, helping them find freedom from great burdens of emotional pain and shame. Through these experiences with others, I have seen firsthand the transforming power of agapē.

Restoring My Soul with God

In their book *How We Love*,[22] authors Milan and Kay Yerkovich offer a practical guide to understanding and applying attachment theory. The book is tailored to marital relationships, but the principles throughout are easily applied to other relationships as well. Milan and Kay provide a free online survey that helps you identify your prominent attachment style and offers helpful strategies for growth (https://howwelove.com/love-style-quiz/). For this exercise, take the "Love Style Quiz" and work through the growth process Milan and Kay suggest. If you are married, I encourage you to have your spouse take the quiz, too, and discuss your findings together.

Restoring My Soul with Others

1. Why must the process of Christ-formation be relational? Isn't our relationship with God enough?

2. Why is loneliness so dangerous?

3. Do you think it is difficult for people to receive God's love unconditionally? Explain.

4. How could the analogy of the vine and the branches (John 15) illustrate the Christ-formation process? What does it mean to abide in Jesus, and what fruit is the result of doing so?

5. Does producing fruit require direct effort on your part, or is it only the work of the Holy Spirit? Discuss.

6. Reflect on the skywriting story. How has God communicated his love for you? What aspects in creation remind you of God's love and presence?

7. Think of a recent experience of receiving safe feedback from a trusted friend. How did their feedback help you? What did it change? In what ways did they respond that were helpful?

8. Describe what you would do to offer safe feedback to a friend.

13

SPIRITUAL DISCIPLINES
TO REWIRE YOUR BRAIN

SPIRITUAL WARFARE IS A BATTLE for your mind, or more specifically, your thoughts. John MacArthur calls it "a battle for the minds of people who are captive to lies that are exalted in opposition to Scripture."[1] Paul uses battle imagery in 2 Corinthians 10:4-5 (NLT):

> We use God's mighty weapons, not worldly weapons, to knock down the strongholds of human reasoning and to destroy false arguments. We destroy every proud obstacle that keeps people from knowing God. We capture their rebellious thoughts and teach them to obey Christ.

The "strongholds" to which Paul refers include the lies and distortions we choose to believe about God and ourselves that promote spiritual/ emotional conflicts. Certain spiritual disciplines—Bible study, biblical meditation, and memorizing Scripture—challenge those strongholds by rewiring our brains with the truths of God's Word. Many believers struggle with the idea of spiritual disciplines because it seems to contradict their understanding of salvation by grace through faith (Ephesians 2:8-9). The concern is this: *If grace is a gift and salvation is not the result of works, how can any effort on my part be biblical?* The answer to this question is important, so let me explain.

Christ-Formation and Personal Effort

Grace is God's unmerited favor unto salvation, as well as God's unmerited power unto Christ-formation. In other words, grace is both the gift of salvation and the power of God that fuels Christ-formation. Consider the biblical evidence in Figure 13.1 below.

FIGURE 13.1

GRACE

UNMERITED FAVOR OF GOD
GRACE IS THE GIFT FROM GOD OF SALVATION

The gift of salvation	Ephesians 2:8-9
The gift of hope	Romans 6:23
The gift of eternal life	2 Thessalonians 2:16
The gift of calling	Galatians 1:15
The gift of justification	Romans 3:24
The gift of the Holy Spirit	Romans 5:5
The gift of life	Romans 6:14
The gift of "all things"	Romans 8:32
The gift of Spiritual Gifts	1 Corinthians 12:7
The gift of life and breath	Acts 17:25

UNMERITED POWER OF GOD
GRACE IS THE POWER OF GOD FOR TRANSFORMATION

Power to work out salvation	Philippians 2:12-13
Power for transformation	2 Corinthians 3:17-18
Power to stand against Satan	Ephesians 6:10
Power to do all things	Philippians 4:13
Power to control my thoughts	2 Corinthians 10:4
Power to endure hardship	2 Corinthians 12:9
Power for life and godliness	2 Peter 1:3
Power for ministry	Romans 1:5, 12:3 1 Corinthians 3:10, Ephesians 3:8, 4:7
Power for strength	2 Timothy 2:1

As you can see, grace is the gift of salvation, specifically the forgiveness of sin that gives birth to new life in Christ and a home in heaven (Ephesians 1:13-14). Salvation encompasses so much more, however: In fact, it involves specific stages and phases, each of which offers an incredible benefit. The stages of salvation include regeneration (2 Corinthians 5:17), justification (Romans 10:9-10; 2 Corinthians 5:21), sanctification (1 Peter 2:9-10), and glorification (1 John 3:2). Sanctification includes its own three phases: positional sanctification (Hebrews 10:10), progressive sanctification (2 Corinthians 3:18), and complete sanctification (1 John 3:2). Progressive sanctification, or Christ-formation, is the *only* aspect of salvation that involves our direct participation. It involves becoming more and more like Jesus Christ in his character and quality of life and is completed in heaven.

And yet, even our direct participation in progressive sanctification is the result of God's grace. Consider Figure 13.2 below.

FIGURE 13.2

Our direct participation with the Holy Spirit in the process of progressive sanctification is important, as the Scriptures demonstrate.

- "Walk by the Spirit . . . let us also keep in step with the Spirit" (Galatians 5:16, 25).

- "Be filled with the Spirit" (Ephesians 5:18).

- "Put off your old self . . . be renewed in the spirit of your minds . . . put on the new self, created after the likeness of God in true righteousness and holiness" (Ephesians 4:22-24).

- "Work out your own salvation with fear and trembling" (Philippians 2:12).

- "What you have learned and received and heard and seen in me—practice these things" (Philippians 4:9).

- "Spend your time and energy in the exercise of keeping spiritually fit. Bodily exercise is all right, but spiritual exercise is much more important and is a tonic for all you do. So exercise yourself spiritually" (1 Timothy 4:7-8, TLB).

- "Make every effort to add to your faith goodness; and to goodness, knowledge; and to knowledge, self-control; and to self-control, perseverance; and to perseverance, godliness; and to godliness, mutual affection; and to mutual affection, love. For if you possess these qualities in increasing measure, they will keep you from being ineffective and unproductive in your knowledge of our Lord Jesus Christ" (2 Peter 1:5-8, NIV).

- "Put away all malice and all deceit and hypocrisy and envy and all slander. Like newborn infants, long for the pure spiritual milk" (1 Peter 2:1-2).

- "Grow in the grace and knowledge of our Lord and Savior Jesus Christ" (2 Peter 3:18).

Our direct participation in progressive sanctification is an important yet often missing ingredient in much of our discipleship literature and programs today. Let's explore how spiritual disciplines facilitate the Christ-formation process.

Grace-Sustained Spiritual Disciplines

Our direct participation in Christ-formation, or progressive sanctification, includes grace-sustained spiritual disciplines. Any spiritual discipline carried out in our own strength cannot facilitate progress in Christ-formation, nor can it lead to a greater experience of the abundant life. And yet, direct participation—empowered by God's grace and carried out in partnership with the Holy Spirit—becomes a powerful catalyst for change. Dallas Willard wrote,

> Christ-likeness of the inner being is not a merely human attainment.
> It is, finally, a gift of grace. The resources for it are not human, but
> come from the interactive presence of the Holy Spirit in the lives of
> those who place their confidence in Christ.[2]

All direct participation that applies to the Christ-formation process must be grace-sustained if it is to produce spiritual/emotional growth and abundant living in Christ. A grace-sustained spiritual discipline cultivates *new thoughts* that promote healthy emotions and *new intentions* that affect the will and drive obedience, which together promote a greater experience of the abundant life.

I like to use a farming analogy to describe our part in Christ-formation. A farmer cannot make a crop grow, but he can create an environment conducive to growth. For example, as the farmer plows the soil and plants, waters, and fertilizes the seed, he creates an environment for growth. Similarly, grace-sustained spiritual disciplines create an environment where spiritual/emotional growth can take place.

For example, we know the Scripture to be God's Word, and we know that the Holy Spirit uses Scripture to transform us into the likeness of Christ. This gracious work of Christ-formation, therefore, necessarily involves making time to read and study the Bible; God does not read the Bible for us.

Let's look now at the grace-sustained spiritual disciplines that can rewire the brain—that is, replace lies and distortions with God's truth.

Bible Study

The English Protestant Bible is composed of 66 books containing 1,189 chapters, 31,102 verses, and roughly 800,000 words.[3] The Bible is a supernatural document inspired by God (2 Timothy 3:16-17; 2 Peter 1:20-21), so it can be trusted as the definitive source for Christ-formation. The Holy Spirit is our guide—as the Spirit of truth (John 16:13)—who helps us understand and apply Scripture to our lives. In order to replace the lies and distorted thoughts in our brains and experience the abundant life that Jesus offers, it's imperative that we cultivate a robust understanding of Scripture. Robert Saucy wrote,

> Spiritual life and growth in all of its aspects thus flows from the knowledge of truth found in the revelation of God. . . . To seek spiritual transformation apart from a steady diet of God's Word is like trying to gain physical strength without eating. Both are impossible.[4]

Studying Scripture enables us to focus our thinking on what God says is true; in this way, God's Word can literally rewire your brain. This rewiring process doesn't happen by accident, nor can it take place overnight, but if you commit to a regular practice of Bible study, the Holy Spirit can use God's Word to renovate your heart.

God's Word is not simply information but revelation and helps us not only to know *about* God but also to *know* God as Father, Son, and Holy Spirit. Eugene Peterson's favorite metaphor for Bible study was "Eat this book," which relates the Word of God to spiritual food that feeds the soul and informs the mind. Peterson maintained that "the Holy Spirit uses them [the Scriptures] to form Christ in us," and that "We are not interested in knowing more but in becoming more."[5] As we study the Bible, we are literally hearing God speak to us, revealing aspects of his nature and character and instructing us in how to live as the people of God.

The Bible informs us on everything we need for faith and practice. Therefore, we must approach Bible study with eagerness, not only to hear what God wants to say to us but to then put his words into action. Obedience is a catalyst for Christ-formation and the abundant life. James 1:22-25 (NLT) says,

> Don't just listen to God's word. You must do what it says. Otherwise, you are only fooling yourselves. For if you listen to the word and don't obey, it is like glancing at your face in a mirror. You see yourself, walk away, and forget what you look like. But if you look carefully into the perfect law that sets you free, and if you do what it says and don't forget what you heard, then God will bless you for doing it.

There are a variety of ways to study the Bible, but one I find helpful is to read a commentary. Commentaries will help you understand the historical context, the theology inherent in the text, and the meanings of words in the original languages. Many commentaries also offer practical ways to apply the truths of Scripture to your life. All Scripture is instructive for Christ-formation (2 Timothy 3:16-17), but two specific categories of biblical truth are especially helpful: the nature and character of God and your identity in Christ. Let's look at these two categories and a few related topics.

Knowing God by His Attributes and Names

How does God work in us to move us toward the abundant life? It's partly a function of his attributes, which reinforce the benefits of his lordship (specifically, the limitations of our circumstances to override God's power and authority). When we reflect regularly on God's attributes, we find ourselves in and moving toward joyful hope and the abundant life that is ours, now, in Christ.

Of God's many attributes, I am especially drawn to his *independence*, that is, God is completely self-sufficient, in need of nothing (Psalm 50:10-12; Acts 17:24-25); his *unchangeableness*, that God remains constant and consistent, the same throughout eternity (Psalm 90:2; 1 Peter 1:24-25); his *eternality*, that God has no beginning and no end (Job 36:26; Revelation 1:8); his *omnipresence*, that God is not limited to time and space (Psalm 139:7-10); his *unity*, that no attribute of God is more important than another—God is both *just* (Acts 17:31) and *compassionate* (Exodus 34:6); and his *omnipotence*, that God is all-powerful (Isaiah 44:24; Jude 1:24-25). Theologian Wayne Grudem refers to God's attributes as "different ways of looking at the totality of God's character."[6]

We also discover various aspects of God's character by studying his names. Throughout the Bible, you will find different names for God that refer to different aspects of his character. Consider the following: *Elohim*: God is creator (Genesis 1:1), *Elohim Chayim*: the living God (Joshua 3:10), *Abba*: God is Father (Romans 8:15), *Jehovah-jireh*: the Lord provides (Genesis 22:9-14), *Jehovah-shalom*: the Lord is peace (Judges 6:22-24), *El Elyon*: God is your sovereign (Psalm 147:5), *El Kanna*: the jealous God (Exodus 34:14), *El Roi*: the God who sees (Genesis 16:13), *Jehovah Rói*: God is your shepherd (Psalm 23:1), *Jehovah Nissi*: God is your banner (Exodus 17:15).[7] There are many other names for God in the Bible, but these ten provide a place to begin a Bible study to help correct any distortions you might have about God.

Knowing God by Biblical Symbolism and Metaphors

Symbols and metaphors are used in the Bible to characterize God. Some of these symbols include the Tabernacle and its furnishings (Exodus 25–31; 35–40; John 2:19-21), the bronze serpent (Numbers 21:6-9; John 3:14-15), and the Old Testament sacrificial system (Leviticus 1–7; Hebrews 10:5-9). These symbols inform an accurate knowledge of God.

In addition, the Bible contains hundreds of metaphors that reveal various aspects of God's character. For example, God is referred to as an eagle (Exodus 19:4), a husband (Isaiah 54:5), a shepherd (Psalm 80:1), a loving father (1 John 3:1), a rock (Psalm 18:2), a fortress (Psalm 91:1-4), a potter

(Jeremiah 18:6), a king (Psalm 47:7), light (1 John 1:5), a great physician (Psalm 103:2-3), fire (Deuteronomy 4:24), and a vinedresser (John 15:1).

Biblical symbols and metaphors enable us to know God in a deeply personal way and can help us rewire our brain using biblical truth.

Knowing God through Jesus Christ and the Holy Spirit

Perhaps one of the best ways to inform our knowledge of God is to study the life and teachings of Jesus Christ, who is the physical manifestation of God: "The Son radiates God's own glory and expresses the very character of God" (Hebrews 1:3, NLT). Jesus stated plainly that if you see him, you see the Father (John 14:9). Studying the life and teachings of Jesus in the Scriptures, therefore, will accurately inform our knowledge of God.

The Holy Spirit is the one who guides us into all truth (John 16:13), including the truth about God. Paul writes, "The Lord—who is the Spirit—makes us more and more like him as we are changed into his glorious image" (2 Corinthians 3:18, NLT). Numerous symbols and metaphors in the Bible inform us about the Holy Spirit. For example, the Holy Spirit is the deposit (Ephesians 1:14) and seal (2 Corinthians 1:22) who guarantees our inheritance in Christ. The Holy Spirit is the author of Scripture (2 Peter 1:21; 2 Timothy 3:16). The Holy Spirit is the comforter, counselor, and advocate who comes alongside all those who belong to Christ (Isaiah 11:2; John 14:16; 15:26; 16:7). The Holy Spirit convicts the world of sin (John 16:7-11), lives in the heart of every believer (Romans 8:9-11; Ephesians 2:21-22; 1 Corinthians 6:19), intercedes for all who belong to Christ (Romans 8:26), is our teacher (John 14:26; 1 Corinthians 2:13), confirms in our hearts that we are God's children (Romans 8:16), and pours God's love into us (Romans 5:5).

In the Bible, the Holy Spirit is referred to as water (Isaiah 44:3; John 7:37-39), oil (Isaiah 61:1; Acts 10:38), fire (Isaiah 4:4; Matthew 3:11-12), and wind (Ezekiel 37:9-14; Acts 2:3). The Holy Spirit generously distributes spiritual gifts to God's people (Romans 12:6-8; 1 Corinthians 12:8-10) to build up the body of Christ (Ephesians 4:11-13) and to serve others (1 Peter 4:11). It is the Holy Spirit who cultivates Christlike character in the heart of every believer (Galatians 5:22-23).

As you study the truth about God in Scripture—Father, Son, and Holy Spirit—you create neuropathways in your brain that will help you replace distortions about God with the truth.

Knowing My Identity in Christ

In Christ, you are a child of God (John 1:12), the salt of the earth (Matthew 5:13), the light of the world (Matthew 5:14), and part of the true vine—that is, Christ (John 15:1). In Christ, you are Jesus' friend (John 15:15), a son or daughter of God (Romans 8:14), and a joint heir with Christ, who shares everything that is his (Romans 8:17). Your body is a temple where the Holy Spirit dwells (1 Corinthians 3:16). In Christ, you are a member of Christ's own body (1 Corinthians 12:27), a "new creation" (2 Corinthians 5:17), a minister of reconciliation (2 Corinthians 5:18-19), a saint (1 Corinthians 1:2; Ephesians 1:1), God's workmanship, "created in Christ Jesus for good works" (Ephesians 2:10), and a partaker of the divine nature (2 Peter 1:4). In Christ, you are declared righteous and holy (Ephesians 4:24), "hidden with Christ in God" (Colossians 3:3), chosen by God and precious to him (1 Peter 2:4). In Christ, you are a son or daughter of light (1 Thessalonians 5:5), seated with Christ in heaven (Ephesians 2:6), one of God's "living stones" (1 Peter 2:5), and a member of "a royal priesthood, a holy nation," a people belonging to God (1 Peter 2:9-10). In Christ, you are an alien and stranger in this world (1 Peter 2:11) and a citizen of heaven (Philippians 3:20). Each aspect of your identity in Christ became true at the moment of salvation.[8]

If you allow the truth of your identity in Christ to replace the lies and distorted thoughts that play on repeat in your mind, you will be able to break free from feelings of shame that keep you stuck. Neil Anderson writes,

> People cannot consistently behave in ways that are inconsistent
> with the way they perceive themselves. . . . If, however, you
> see yourself as a child of God who is spiritually alive in Christ,
> you will begin to live accordingly. Next to a knowledge of God,
> a knowledge of who you are is by far the most important truth
> you can possess.[9]

As you study what the Bible says about who you are in Christ, the Holy Spirit will use those truths to replace the lies that drive the spiritual/emotional conflicts that hinder your Christ-formation.

Biblical Meditation

The second grace-sustained spiritual discipline that reinforces God's truth in your heart is meditating on Scripture. Meditation is an important way to wire God's truth in your brain. One of the main Hebrew words used in the Old Testament for meditation is *sikah* (or the verb form *siakh*). Saucy defines *siakh* as

> rehearsing or going over something in one's mind, either outwardly talking or musing silently . . . *siakh* refers to pondering on God's Word so that it dominates our mind and heart and becomes the perspective through which we view all of life and the world around us.[10]

Meditating on Scripture has been a biblically sound practice for centuries.

Many Christians are afraid of the word *meditation*, so let's be clear about what I mean. Biblical meditation is a "conscious, continuous engagement of the mind with God."[11] You practice biblical meditation as you ponder God's Word. Old Testament scholars Edward Curtis and John Brugaletta explain the importance of meditating on God's Word for transformation:

> What a person regularly thinks about strongly influences what he or she does and, in many instances, also determines what the person becomes. . . .
>
> Meditation helps focus the attention on things that are consistent with God's order and thus helps to produce behavior and character that are consistent with God's truth.[12]

We see this understanding of meditation throughout Scripture, especially in the Psalms of David and the book of Joshua. Consider the following:

- "This Book of the Law shall not depart from your mouth, but you shall meditate on it day and night, so that you may be careful to do according to all that is written in it" (Joshua 1:8).

- "Blessed is the man who walks not in the counsel of the wicked, nor stands in the way of sinners, nor sits in the seat of scoffers; but his delight is in the law of the LORD, and on his law he meditates day and night" (Psalm 1:1-2).

- "I will meditate on your precepts" (Psalm 119:15, 78).

- "I will meditate on your wondrous works" (Psalm 119:27).

- "I will meditate on your statutes" (Psalm 119:48).

- "Oh how I love your law! It is my meditation all the day" (Psalm 119:97).

- "Your testimonies are my meditation" (Psalm 119:99).

- "My eyes are awake before the watches of the night, that I may meditate on your promise" (Psalm 119:148).

We find different ways to practice biblical meditation in the pages of Scripture. Moses said to the Israelites,

> You must commit yourselves wholeheartedly to these commands that I am giving you today. Repeat them again and again to your children. Talk about them when you are at home and when you are on the road, when you are going to bed and when you are getting up. Tie them to your hands and wear them on your forehead as reminders. Write them on the doorposts of your house and on your gates.
>
> DEUTERONOMY 6:6-9, NLT

The Lord commanded every king of Israel to write out God's law by his own hand and keep this written record with him to read every day:

> When he sits on the throne of his kingdom, he shall write for himself in a book a copy of this law, approved by the Levitical priests. And it shall be with him, and he shall read in it all the days of his life, that he may learn to fear the Lord his God by keeping all the words of this law and these statutes, and doing them.
>
> DEUTERONOMY 17:18-19

David wrote in Psalm 1:1-2 that meditating on God's Word produces an abundant life:

> Oh, the joys of those who do not
>> follow the advice of the wicked,
>> or stand around with sinners,
>> or join in with mockers.
> But they delight in the law of the LORD,
>> meditating on it day and night.
> They are like trees planted along the riverbank,
>> bearing fruit each season.
> Their leaves never wither,
>> and they prosper in all they do.
>
> PSALM 1:1-2, NLT

Having studied passages about the attributes of God, consider just sitting with the text, reading it over and over—even out loud—taking note of any words or phrases that jump out to you and considering those words to be God speaking directly to you (John 10:27-28; Romans 10:17). Think of biblical meditation as another way to ingest God's Word: "When your words showed up, I ate them—swallowed them whole. What a feast!" (Jeremiah 15:16, MSG).

Memorizing Scripture

As important and helpful as both Bible study and biblical meditation are to Christ-formation, memorizing Scripture might be the single most effective way to rewire your brain. Dallas Willard wrote,

> Bible memorization is absolutely fundamental to spiritual formation. If I had to choose between all the disciplines of the spiritual life, I would choose Bible memorization, because it is a fundamental way of filling our minds with what it needs.[13]

Most people I coach in Christ-formation are intimidated to memorize Scripture. When I suggest it as a spiritual discipline, the automatic response is to say, "Oh, I could never do that." I have often wondered if this resistance is due to the fact that memorizing Scripture will produce the greatest results and is therefore susceptible to greater spiritual attack.

A few years ago, my wife decided to memorize the entire book of Ephesians. Yes, you read that right—all 6 chapters, 155 verses, and roughly 2,422 words. It took her two years, but she did it, and the transformation I saw in her life as a result was profound. She developed a greater sense of security in her identity in Christ, a greater confidence in God's love and presence, and an increased capacity to challenge the lies and distortions about God and herself that resulted from abuse she experienced in childhood.

Frankly, I was so inspired by the changes I saw in Susan that I decided to start memorizing more Scripture too. Over the last five years, I have memorized Colossians 3:1-17, Ephesians 1:18-19 and 3:14-19, 2 Peter 1:3-11, Psalm 23, and Isaiah 40:28-31. These have become my go-to passages when I find myself stuck in a loop of negative thinking, doubt, and worry.

Today, I have quick access to God's truth whenever I feel afraid. The Holy Spirit affirms the truth of God's Word that I have hidden in my heart and brings from it both comfort and strength. Even presently, when I wake up in the middle of the night gripped by fear, I have trained myself to immediately recite the passages of Scripture I have memorized. Before I know it, I'm waking up the next morning.

It is an amazing phenomenon that the brain can only focus on one thought at a time. That means you cannot be afraid and at peace at the same time; you can only experience one or the other in the present moment. I often remind people that multitasking is a myth. It's true that you can shift between thoughts very quickly, but it is not possible to think a negative thought and a positive thought at the same time. If you choose to think about whatever is true, noble, right, pure, admirable, and praiseworthy (Philippians 4:8), you can't also be thinking about the many terrible things that could happen to you. I have discovered that when I focus my attention on Scripture, I find that peace and hope quickly replace any fear and dread. I love Isaiah 26:3: "You will keep in perfect peace all who trust in you, all whose thoughts are *fixed* on you" (NLT, emphasis added).

Even though I'm extolling the benefits of memorizing Scripture, my guess is, it might still intimidate you. That's why I have come up with a way to memorize Scripture by accident.

How to Memorize Scripture by Accident

Full disclosure: You can't memorize Scripture by accident; it does take effort. But if you put the following steps into practice, you will discover that it's a lot easier than you think. These are the steps that I use to memorize Scripture, so I know they work and can help you.

Memorize Passages Rather Than Single Verses

Memorizing a long passage helps you keep what you're memorizing in its context. The flow of the text aides the memorizing process. Many Scripture memorization plans are organized topically, which is fine, but it can also be more difficult, since the memorized verses don't flow together naturally. Also, context is important for rightly interpreting Scripture, so memorizing a verse in isolation from its context can lead to misunderstanding and misapplication of the truth in it. By memorizing passages, you are much less likely to misapply the verse because you retain the context.

Study the Passage You Are Memorizing

Study tools like commentaries or study Bibles can help you understand a passage of Scripture. Moreover, additional concentration on the passage anchors it in your memory. Remember Hebb's law: "Neurons that fire together, wire together." In other words, the more ways you concentrate on a Bible passage, the more thoroughly that truth will be etched into your brain and the more direct access you will have to it.

Write Out the Passage

Handwriting passages further reinforces the memorization process. As you write, you continue to strengthen neuropathways that facilitate long-term memory. You may be tempted to type the text on a computer, but I advise against that because the physical experience of handwriting is more impactful on the memorization process than typing.

When I begin memorizing a new passage, I like to write down each verse on a separate 3 × 5 card. On one side of the card, I write down the reference, and on the other side, I write the verse. I know this sounds old school, but it works. The cards are easy to carry around in my pocket, put in the glove box in my truck, or tape to the mirror in my bathroom. When

Susan was memorizing Ephesians, she taped dozens of these note cards to our bathroom mirror (so many, in fact, that at times, I could hardly see my reflection).

Especially if I'm memorizing a longer passage like Colossians 3:1-17, I sit down every few days and write out as much of the passage as I can remember. This reinforces what I have already memorized but also helps me to identify words that I have forgotten.

Because 3 × 5 cards are easy to misplace, I also like to type the verses into an app on my cell phone. This keeps everything in one place and makes reviewing the passage easy.[14] Once I have a passage memorized, I like to review it periodically to keep it fresh.

Review the Passage Three Times a Day

The more often you review a passage, the more deeply you encode it to memory. I recommend reviewing your 3 × 5 cards a minimum of three times a day. You might even want to write out multiple copies of your note cards so you can keep them handy in different places—next to your bed so you can review them the first thing in the morning and right before you go to sleep, at your workspace so you can review them throughout the day, and in your purse or backpack so you can review them during your lunch break. If you read through your 3 × 5 cards three times a day for thirty days, you will have reviewed the passage over ninety times; the repetition alone will help you memorize the passage.

Recite the Passage Out Loud

I'm often surprised at how hard it is to recite a passage out loud, especially in front of others, even when I have it memorized. It's easy to get distracted when I'm looking at people or when I hear myself repeat the verses out loud. But I recommend making this part of your memorizing strategy. Say the verses out loud when you're driving in your car. People might look at you funny when you pull up to a stoplight, but who cares—it works.

Record Yourself Reading the Passage

I recommend recording yourself reading your notecards and listening to them when you're driving or exercising. Make sure you read the passage slowly, so you can concentrate on specific words and phrases.

Expect Resistance

Memorizing Scripture takes effort because it requires focused attention. But whatever effort it takes, it's worth it. Memorizing Scripture might be the most important spiritual discipline you can practice for Christ-formation.

Satan doesn't want you to renew your mind (Romans 12:1-2); he wants you to continue believing lies and rehearsing negative and distorted thoughts in your mind, so expect resistance. Satan will throw everything at you to discourage you from memorizing Scripture. But don't give in to him. Try it for the next thirty days—work on memorizing a passage that is important to you. I think you will discover that if you put these steps into practice, you will memorize Scripture by accident (well, almost).

In this chapter, we discussed three spiritual disciplines the Holy Spirit can use to rewire your brain toward Christ-formation and abundant living. Grace-sustained spiritual disciplines such as Bible study, biblical meditation, and memorizing Scripture will help you "take every thought captive to obey Christ" (2 Corinthians 10:5). In the next chapter, we'll explore four additional spiritual disciplines that can help your Christ-formation.

Restoring My Soul with God

Because memorizing Scripture is so intimidating, let's just take the bull by the horns and go after it. Colossians 3:1-17 has been an important passage for me over the last five years. As you memorize it, consider the following suggestions:

1. Use a more literal translation such as the English Standard Version (ESV); the New King James Version (NKJV); the New International Version (NIV); the New American Standard Version (NASB), or the New Living Translation (NLT). If you prefer to use a paraphrase like *The Passion* (TPT), *The Voice* (VOICE), or *The Living Bible* (TLB), that's fine too. Bible Gateway is a free online tool that includes dozens of different translations and paraphrases you can use: http://www .biblegateway.com.

2. If you don't have a study Bible, I encourage you to buy one. The introduction for each book, the notes at the bottom of the page, and other tools are invaluable. I recommend a *Life Application Study Bible* (in the translation of your choice) or *The Renovaré Spiritual Formation Study Bible*.

3. Study the passage using a commentary. For Colossians, I recommend Warren Wiersbe's *BE Complete*.[15] Dr. Wiersbe's commentaries are excellent—and easy to follow and understand.

4. I also encourage you to read James Bryan Smith's book *Hidden in Christ*,[16] which is focused on the various aspects of Colossians 3:1-17. It will help you understand various nuances in the text that will assist you in the memorizing process.

Follow my "How to Memorize Scripture by Accident" process in this chapter. You can do this!

Restoring My Soul with Others

1. Share about your experience so far in memorizing Colossians 3:1-17. What steps in the section "How to Memorize Scripture by Accident" are you finding most helpful?

2. After reading this chapter, does it make sense that there is no conflict between grace and direct effort for our part in Christ-formation?

3. Review the salvation diagram (Figure 13.2). Why is it important to understand that salvation is about so much more than forgiveness of sin and going to heaven when you die?

4. Why is progressive sanctification the only phase that requires our direct participation?

5. What has been your experience with spiritual disciplines? How would you explain to someone that they are not legalistic? (Consider the farming analogy in this chapter.)

6. Which of the three spiritual disciplines in this chapter—Bible study, biblical meditation, Scripture memorization—are you most interested in pursuing? Why? Which discipline are you most intimidated to try? Discuss.

7. Do you know Christians who think all forms of meditation are wrong? Based on the information in this chapter, how could you help them understand a biblical definition of this discipline?

8. Based on your growing understanding of the brain, why do you think Dallas Willard believed that memorizing Scripture was the most important spiritual discipline? What do *you* think?

9. Which biblical symbol or metaphor resonates with you the most? Why? Which are you curious about? Are there other metaphors in Scripture you can think of that were not listed?

10. We have talked a lot about the importance of understanding our identity in Christ. Why do you think that is so important to Christ-formation?

14

SPIRITUAL DISCIPLINES
TO HEAL THE HEART

THROUGHOUT THIS BOOK, we have identified spiritual/emotional conflicts as distorted beliefs about God, self, and others. These distortions promote toxic emotions, including shame, fear, anger, sadness, hopeless despair, and disgust. In order to resolve these emotional conflicts, we must replace the lies that promote hurt and shame with the truth about God and our identity in Christ. This is done in partnership with the Holy Spirit and in relationships with others we trust to give us safe feedback. The grace-sustained spiritual disciplines that help heal the heart include solitude, prayer, silence, and confession.

Solitude: Time Alone with God
In *solitude*, we invite the Holy Spirit to examine our hearts. Henri Nouwen describes solitude as the "furnace of transformation" because while in solitude, we are better able to give God our full attention.[1] You can find solitude by walking in the park, along the beach, or around the block. I can even experience solitude sitting quietly in my backyard. When making space for

solitude, the most important thing to keep in mind is finding a place as free of distractions as possible.

Times of solitude provide the opportunity to invite the Holy Spirit to expose any hurts in our hearts that need to be identified and processed. Spiritual director Adele Calhoun explains,

> When no one is there to watch, judge and interpret what we say, the Spirit often brings us face to face with hidden motives and compulsions. . . .
>
> Alone, without distractions, we put ourselves in a place where God can reveal things to us that we might not notice in the normal preoccupations of life.[2]

No matter how many years have passed, God remembers all our hurts and understands our pain. David writes, "You keep track of all my sorrows. You have collected all my tears in your bottle. You have recorded each one in your book" (Psalm 56:8, NLT). It's comforting to know not only how much God really cares but also how much he wants to heal my wounded heart (Psalm 147:3). Emotional pain must be exposed in order to be processed; that's why we need to find a quiet place, free of distractions, where we attune to God.

Prayer: Listening to God

Years ago, I was taught to pray according to the acronym ACTS (adoration, confession, thanksgiving, and supplication). Adoration includes praising God for who he is in his nature and character. Confession involves bringing any known sin to God and asking for his forgiveness. Thanksgiving is taking time to express my gratitude to God for specific things he has done or is doing in my life. Supplication is making my request(s) known to God.

While I think ACTS as a model for prayer is fine, it seems to be missing a vital ingredient: to listen. In order to have a conversation with a person, including God, both parties need to be sharing and listening. *Prayer* is a dialogue between you and God, not a monologue. Therefore, in prayer, you need to listen to God speak to you.

Sometimes I need to listen for God's discipline or direction in my life. At other times, I need God to reveal hurt or hurtful ways in me that need to be confessed. And many times, I need to hear God say, "Ken, I love you, and I am so glad to spend this time with you." Consider David's prayer in Psalm 139:23-24 as a model: "Search me, God, and know my heart; test me and know my anxious thoughts. See if there is any offensive way in me" (NIV). David was asking God to reveal anything in his heart that might negatively affect his relationship with God or others. This is a powerful process that can bring greater awareness of what is going on in the deep places in my heart as well as a prayer to become more aware of God's presence. Many times, while in solitude, God has revealed a hurt that I was avoiding but he wanted to process with me. I have witnessed God's loving presence in times of solitude both in my own life and in the lives of others.

Since 2011, I have been on a team that leads small cohorts of men through a five-day discipleship experience called the Trinity Encounter hosted at Trinity Ranch in Montana. Trinity Ranch is a two thousand-acre working cattle ranch, featuring lush fields of alfalfa, acres of towering pine trees, and local wildlife (including deer, elk, eagles, and the occasional sighting of a scrawny black bear): It is a western paradise. The ranch is far removed from "civilization" and the normal distractions of urban life. There's no Starbucks, In-N-Out Burger, or 5-star hotel, but the accommodations are excellent and the food is great. Daily routine includes teaching sessions, small-group time, and numerous opportunities to be alone with God, surrounded by the beauty of his creation. Throughout the week, we encourage the men to invite the Holy Spirit to examine their hearts to reveal any "anxious thoughts" or "offensive way[s]."

Over the years, I have witnessed hundreds of men experience a personal and intimate encounter with God. Some of them, for the first time in a long time, slowed down enough to hear the "gentle whisper" of the Spirit (1 Kings 19:12, NIV). Many find freedom from shame that has bogged them down for years as they process past hurt and confess sin. It's not that these men needed to come to Montana to find God—God is always near—but that God called them to Montana to make space for him to work.

Silence: Listening for God to Speak

In order to better hear the voice of God, we need to be as free from distractions as possible. I believe God is always speaking to us, but we are not always listening. *Silence* gives us the time to dial our hearts to the frequency of God's voice.

Sometimes God will speak to you by bringing to mind a memory of a hurtful event that you have not thought about in years. He might even bring to mind a person who hurt you. At other times, God may speak to you through a verse of Scripture or remind you of a story from the Bible. When you are waiting for God to speak, the important thing is to be quiet and wait.

A few years ago, I fell and broke my wrist; it was a painful and difficult ordeal. I broke my wrist on a Friday, and my doctor recommended immediate surgery. I was scheduled to leave for a Trinity Encounter on Sunday, however, so I told my doctor that the surgery would have to wait. My doctor said the tendons in my arm would begin pulling my wrist bones farther apart, making for a much more difficult surgery. I told him I understood but respectfully refused and asked him to put my arm in a cast. There was no way I was going to miss a Trinity Encounter to be a part of what God was going to do in the lives of men that week. I promised my doctor that I would schedule surgery immediately upon my return. He reluctantly agreed and put my arm in a cast. The pain was tolerable, but the cast made life incredibly inconvenient.

When I arrived at the airport on Sunday morning to catch my flight for Montana, I stood in line at Starbucks to buy coffee, which is a normal part of my traveling routine. I had forgotten that I only had one working hand, so I couldn't hold my coffee and pull my carry-on-bag at the same time. A stranger, seeing my predicament, asked if he could carry my coffee to my gate. I was embarrassed but accepted his offer.

After I boarded the plane, I was faced with another dilemma: How do I put my heavy carry-on bag in the overhead bin with one hand? As I stood there trying to figure out what to do, another good Samaritan offered to help. Again, I swallowed my pride and accepted. To be honest, I was surprised that two complete strangers would be so quick to offer unsolicited help; it almost restored my lost confidence in humanity.

The rest of my trip was uneventful—until I woke up the next morning. When I got out of bed and started to dress myself, I realized there were some things I could not do alone. I couldn't tie my shoes, buckle my belt, or put on my watch (don't laugh; you try doing all that with one hand). I had to face the fact that I was going to need to ask for help the entire week. Thankfully, one of the other pastors I was sharing a house with was a close friend and was more than willing to help me do those things I couldn't do by myself. (I never got over the humiliation I felt when he buckled my belt!)

You might have picked up on the fact that I have a problem asking other people for help. I love helping others, but I'm resistant to letting other people help me. Later that week, during some time alone with God in solitude, prayer, and silence, I asked him to show me what was behind my resistance. Was it pride? Did asking for help make me feel weak and vulnerable? Was it a control issue on my part?

I was fully expecting God to say sternly, "all the above," but as I sat quietly and listened, a phrase came to mind: "Nothing is wasted." As I pondered those words and asked God for insight, I began to realize that he was giving me the opportunity—with my broken wrist—to make myself vulnerable and face my fear of rejection by asking others for help.

This was a good lesson and a growth opportunity for me. To this day, I end every email with my name and the phrase the Lord gave me that day: "Nothing is wasted." I can't tell you how many times, over the last few years, people have asked me to explain the story behind that simple phrase. God has used it—time and again—to help people remember that he is in control of everything and can use anything—even a broken wrist—to bring about his glory and our good.

I wonder if God would have spoken to me in the same way if I had never taken that time to be alone with him. I think he would have, but I'm not so sure I would have heard him. Regardless, I believe that the Holy Spirit worked through my pain and a time of solitude, prayer, and silence to continue the work of my Christ-formation.

The Holy Spirit is always ready, willing, and able to meet you where you are. You don't have to travel to Trinity Ranch to have an encounter with God. But if you want to join us, we would love to have you. Time alone with God in solitude, listening prayer, and silence creates a rich environment for Christ-formation.

Confession: Sharing My Hurts with Others

The final spiritual discipline for healing the heart is *confession*. In my experience, most people think of confession as agreeing with God that what we did was wrong and asking for his forgiveness. John writes, "If we confess our sins, he is faithful and just to forgive us our sins and to cleanse us from all unrighteousness" (1 John 1:9). This is an accurate understanding of confession, but like grace, this spiritual discipline includes so much more. We are to confess our sin, but we are also to confess our emotional pain.

James urges all believers to pay attention to the suffering of others within the body of Christ: "Is anyone among you suffering?" (James 5:13). The Greek word for "suffering" is *kakopatheō*, which can refer to either physical or emotional pain. New Testament scholar D. Edmond Hiebert explained the dual meaning of this Greek word when he wrote,

> The term means primarily to endure hardship, to experience some misfortune or calamity. Such suffering what is bad need not be limited to physical suffering; it is a general term that may include trouble and distress as well as sickness.[3]

It's not a stretch to apply this suffering to emotional pain. Bible commentators John Walvoord and Roy Zuck write, "A mutual concern for one another is the way to combat discouragement and downfall. The cure is in personal confession and prayerful concern. The healing is not bodily healing but healing of the soul."[4] Therefore, we can expand confession to be part of the process to resolve the emotional pain that hinders Christ-formation. First, you identify the hurt by listening to God in solitude, prayer, and silence, and then you share (confess) it to others, ideally another believer, who will be an ambassador of Christ to you by offering safe feedback. Paul exhorts believers to "weep with those who weep" (Romans 12:15) and "encourage one another and build one another up" (1 Thessalonians 5:11). This emotional support is a practical way to "carry each other's burdens" (Galatians 6:2, NIV). The Holy Spirit works through human agency to provide the necessary emotional support we need to process the hurts of life.

The specific act of confession that I am referring to for this process involves sharing the circumstances surrounding the painful experience, including the details of what happened, your age at the time of the event, who was involved, and the difficulties it created for you. The goal is not to fix blame or to cause further trauma but to identify and share everything you can remember. Sharing your story like this with a trusted friend opens the door to the grieving process that is essential for resolving the spiritual/emotional conflicts that hinder Christ-formation.

The process of confession sounds simple and straightforward, but it takes courage to ask for help and support from someone else. It is a difficult process but yields substantial results as it helps remove barriers that hinder Christ-formation.

Spiritual Disciplines Help Heal Your Pain

The spiritual disciplines we've discussed so far in this book are not the only ones that can help facilitate the process of Christ-formation, but they are essential and will provide a good place for you to begin as you partner with the Holy Spirit and others to help heal your pain.

The final grace-sustained spiritual discipline that furthers healing and the process of Christ-formation is *forgiveness*. In order to become more like Jesus, we must learn how to forgive others for the hurt they have caused. Hanging on to the hurt only creates resentment and bitterness that poisons the soul.

In the next chapter, I will discuss the essential role of forgiveness in the process of resolving spiritual/emotional conflicts that hinder Christ-formation and the greater experience of the abundant life.

Restoring My Soul with God

For the next five days, I want to invite you to spend three 5-minute blocks of time each day to practice solitude, silence, and listening prayer. Think of this as a spiritual workout and the disciplines as exercises. Paul wrote to Timothy, his young apprentice, "Spend your time and energy in the exercise of keeping spiritually fit. Bodily exercise is all right, but spiritual exercise is much more important and is a tonic for all you do" (1 Timothy 4:7-8, TLB).

1. Find a quiet place where you will not be disturbed. Take out a piece of paper. Acknowledge to Jesus that you know he is sitting next to you and pray, "Search me, God, and know my heart; test me and know my anxious thoughts. See if there is any offensive way in me" (Psalm 139:23-24, NIV).

2. Set a timer for five minutes. Ask Jesus to speak to you. Write down whatever comes to mind, resisting the temptation to judge your thoughts. If you are having difficulty, tell Jesus this is hard and ask him to bring to mind things that he wants to say to you.

3. Reset the timer for five minutes. Test what you wrote down against your knowledge of Scripture. For example, if you heard Jesus say, "I'm so frustrated and disappointed in you; you keep falling into the same sin over and over again. When are you going to stop sinning and follow me?" you know that is not God speaking to you. Scripture says, "There is therefore now no condemnation for those who are in Christ Jesus" (Romans 8:1), and to Moses, God revealed himself as "The LORD, the LORD, a God merciful and gracious, slow to anger, and abounding in steadfast love and faithfulness" (Exodus 34:6). You can also use the Bible to confirm what Jesus said to you. For example, if you heard Jesus say, "I know you struggle with the same sin again and again. And I want you to know I see the struggle in your heart (Psalm 44:21) and I will forgive your sincere repentance (Psalm 51:17; 1 John 1:9) again and again (Matthew 18:21-22). Focus on following me, and I will help you with your sin," you can trust these messages because they are affirmed in the Bible.

4. Reset the timer for five minutes. Thank Jesus for speaking to your heart. Ask him how he wants you to apply his words to your life today. Pay attention to his response.

On the sixth day, share something Jesus said to you with a trusted friend who can offer you safe feedback. When sharing, be specific about what God said, how you heard him say it (e.g., tenderly, with compassion, etc.), any Scripture that came to mind to confirm his word, and how what he said made you feel.

Restoring My Soul with Others

1. If you feel comfortable, share with your group your experience with the five-day "Restoring My Soul with God" exercises.

2. What details from this chapter caught your attention?

3. Is it difficult for you to be alone with God? Where do you feel most comfortable spending time with God?

4. What is the most common way you pray? How could you add time to that to listen to what God wants to say back to you? Do you believe that "prayer is a dialogue between you and God, not a monologue"? Discuss.

5. What is the most effective way to test if it is God speaking to your heart?

6. How would you explain why it's important to spend time alone with God?

15

THE ROLE OF FORGIVENESS
IN CHRIST-FORMATION

DURING THE WEEKS FOLLOWING my termination as a senior pastor, I was not thinking about forgiving the people who had hurt me; instead, I found myself nursing a grudge that was turning into resentment and bitterness. My thinking was locked on to a negative narrative that I was a victim. When a friend would ask me how I was doing, I would reply, "I feel like I was shot in the head and kicked out the door onto the street." Or, "I feel like I've been broadsided by a semitruck." These negative thoughts produced a damaging array of emotions, including hurt, anger, sadness, shame, and fear.

If those feelings weren't bad enough, this experience triggered profound feelings of abandonment and rejection. I thought I had processed my childhood trauma but came to find out that healing takes place in stages; it's like peeling leaves off an artichoke: Aspects of my childhood experiences were still lingering in my heart.

The more I engaged in this negative thinking, the deeper I sank into despair. I just couldn't envision a future where things would ever be the same again. I was experiencing an emotional version of what aviators refer to as a "graveyard spiral." This is a state of disorientation when a pilot doesn't realize they are turning and overcorrects into a rapid descent that ends in a fiery crash. The trauma I was experiencing was causing major disorientation. My world had just been turned upside down, and the more I let the reality of this situation set in, the angrier and more afraid I became. If my descent wasn't adjusted quickly, I was headed for a crash.

Initially, I wasn't angry with God. I wasn't pounding on the door of heaven screaming, "Why God, why? What did I do to deserve this? Why did you let this happen to me?" Instead, my anger was directed toward those who had hurt me—that is, until God spoke to me in prayer one morning. What he said not only took me by surprise but really ticked me off.

I was sitting on the beach by my house early one morning, trying to sort out with God the details of my termination. I remember that morning well; it was still dark, and I was alone. There were no surfers to watch, no dolphins playing beyond the break, and no pelicans dive-bombing for their breakfast to distract me from my thoughts. I was worried about what people in our community were thinking about me because of my abrupt departure: *How many senior pastors leave a church they have served at for over ten years without even saying goodbye?* It just didn't look good; I was afraid it left the impression that I had done something terribly wrong, something that required immediate termination. It's true that I had been struggling in my leadership and that this had caused a fair amount of angst with my pastoral team. In addition to my leadership challenges, I was in regular conflict with three elders, who thought the books my wife and I were reading and recommending to others—on topics of spiritual formation and soul-care—were controversial. This conflict produced a great amount of heartache for me and my wife because our only desire was to help the people in the congregation grow in Christ and experience the greater degree of abundant life that we were finding.

You can survive a few paper cuts, but after a thousand, you will bleed out. Figuratively speaking, it felt like I was bleeding out. No matter how much sleep or how many days off I had, I just couldn't snap back.

Today, I know that these symptoms are signs of burnout, a very real and frequent condition many pastors face.[1] As I look back on that season of my life today, I realize I had been spiraling down into burnout a few years prior to my termination. My wife knew I was running on fumes and she tried to help me see it, but I was too stubborn and afraid to slow down; I thought I could handle it.

During the years I was a senior pastor, I thought I had given the church my very best. As I've heard it said, "I left it all on the field." I gave that church ten of the best years of my life, and yet when I hit the wall, when I needed help, it felt like the elders just put me out, like you take out the trash. From *my* perspective, the harsh treatment and eventual termination were unmerited and unrighteous, and that morning, sitting on the beach, I was angry. I thought I had the right to be outraged about my situation; that is, until God told me otherwise.

I know it was God speaking because the thoughts that came to my mind were not something I ever would have come up with on my own. *Ken, I want you to begin a reconciliation process with the elders . . .*

I didn't even let God finish his sentence; I immediately reacted. *Are you kidding me, God? Are you serious? The elders hurt me! My pastoral staff betrayed me. They need to ask for my forgiveness, not the other way around. You need to read your e-mail, God, because you've got this thing all wrong.*

Of course, God wasn't intimidated by my angry outburst, nor did he strike me dead with a lightning bolt for my insolence. Instead, he started over and spoke to my heart, gently but firmly, saying, *Ken, I want you to begin a reconciliation process with the elders by sending each man a text message humbly asking if he will meet with you so you can apologize for your part in the process that led to your termination. Tell each elder that you have no other agenda.*

That was it—end of transmission. God had spoken, and I just sat there dumbfounded. God's request made no sense to me because I was the victim in this situation. But as I sat there pondering all of this, I knew God was right. In fact, the longer I sat there and thought about it, the more I realized I needed to own up to my part in causing the train wreck.

But this was hard. I don't know about you, but for me, sometimes knowing what to do and then doing it are two very different things.

As I look back on that conversation with God, I realize now that I was harboring a ton of bitterness in my heart—feeding it with the distorted thought that I was a victim—and it was eating me alive. I was in an emotional graveyard spiral, and God was taking the control wheel to adjust my attitude before I crashed. I am thankful for forgiveness: He forgave me for the bitterness I was holding in my heart and gave me the grace to forgive the elders and staff who had hurt me. But genuine forgiveness can't be mechanical—it's not enough to just say the words, "I forgive you"—it's more than an act of the will, it's a matter of the heart.

Whole-Hearted Forgiveness

Genuine forgiveness is the result of a whole-hearted process informed by Scripture (thoughts), motivated by gratitude (feelings), activated by the will (decision), and empowered by grace (the work of the Holy Spirit). Let me explain how this forgiveness process works.

Informed by Scripture

Your thoughts are under your control; as such, you can choose how you think about forgiveness. The whole-hearted forgiveness process begins with thinking about forgiveness *biblically*. That takes us to one of Jesus' most instructive parables about forgiveness.

One day, Peter asked Jesus how many times he should forgive a brother who sinned against him. Before Jesus could even respond, Peter suggested an answer: "Up to seven times?" (Matthew 18:21, NIV). I'm not sure if Peter's question was sincere or if he was looking for Jesus' approval for being so generous. At any rate, I'm pretty sure that Jesus' answer surprised him. "I tell you, not seven times, but seventy-seven times" (Matthew 18:22, NIV).

Why did Peter think seven times was enough? How in the world did he come up with that number? Jewish teaching of the day held that you needed to forgive the same person for the same offense three times. You could liken their thinking to "three strikes and you're out" in our day. In other words, after three times, you have fulfilled your obligation to forgive your brother. This teaching was cited from Old Testament passages, including Amos 1:3-13 and Job 33:29, where it appears that God would forgive Israel's enemies a total of three times before dropping his hammer of judgment.

Jesus' understanding of forgiveness was very different from contemporary Jewish teaching. Jesus taught that genuine forgiveness could never be a matter of law but only of grace. To forgive was more than an act of the will, it required a certain condition of the heart. To reinforce his point, Jesus told the parable of the unmerciful servant.

The parable begins with a servant who owes the king an enormous amount of money. In our day, the amount would be the equivalent to billions of dollars—a sum so large it could never be repaid. The king orders the servant and his entire family to be sold to recoup at least some of the debt. The servant is distraught and falls to his knees begging for mercy. Moved with compassion, the King forgives the *entire* debt.

You would think after experiencing such an astonishing act of mercy, this servant would be so grateful that he would eagerly extend mercy to others. And yet, sadly, the heart of this servant has been unchanged by the generosity of the king. He runs into a man who owes him a sum of money that was a pittance compared to the debt he had owed to the king. When confronted about paying his debt, the second servant falls to his knees and begs for mercy. But instead of extending the same mercy he had received from the king, the forgiven servant assaults this man—literally, grabbing him by the throat—and then has him thrown into prison.

What a tragic outcome, right? Oh, but this is not the end of the story. It seems other servants of the king witness the forgiven servant's shocking lack of mercy and report it. The king is outraged by the news and confronts the forgiven servant: "'You wicked servant,' he said, 'I canceled all that debt of yours because you begged me to. Shouldn't you have had mercy on your fellow servant just as I had on you?'" (Matthew 18:32-33, NIV). Because of the servant's unwillingness to show mercy, the king reinstates the debt in full and throws the man into prison to be tortured by the jailers until he can pay it all back.

Jesus concludes the parable by saying, "This is how my heavenly Father will treat each of you unless you forgive your brother or sister from your heart" (Matthew 18:35, NIV). What is Jesus saying here? He's making the point that those who have been forgiven their debt of sin—a debt they could never repay—should be so grateful that they're eager to forgive others who sin against them.

The moral of Jesus' parable provides a biblical way to think about whole-hearted forgiveness. All of us are like the first servant in Jesus' parable in that our debt of sin is impossible to repay. God—like the king in Jesus' parable—showed us unprecedented mercy and kindness by accepting Jesus' death on the cross as payment in full for our sin. The more we allow the truth about our debt of sin to inform our thinking about forgiveness, the more eager we should be to forgive others when they sin against us.

This teaching on forgiveness is not intended to minimize the hurt we experience when someone sins against us, but it does put our need to forgive them into perspective: We are to forgive others as we have been forgiven (Ephesians 4:32). We can develop this desire to forgive others as we cultivate a heart of gratitude to God for forgiving us.

Motivated by Gratitude

One way to cultivate a heart of gratitude is to reflect on the truth of what Jesus has saved us *from* and what he has saved us *for*.

JESUS SAVED US FROM THE SECOND DEATH

According to the Bible, the first death is physical and a consequence for sin. Paul writes, "When Adam sinned, sin entered the world. Adam's sin brought death, so death spread to everyone, for everyone sinned" (Romans 5:12, NLT). The second death is referred to in the Bible as spiritual death. This, too, is a consequence for sin: It results in an eternal state of separation from God that is so horrible, it is hard to discuss. And yet, in order to fully appreciate God's forgiveness of our sin, we must understand what the Bible teaches about the horrible reality of the second death.

In Revelation 20:15, John refers to the second death as the "lake of fire," a place reserved exclusively for Satan (the Antichrist and false prophet) and the people throughout human history who have rejected God's gift of salvation through his Son, Jesus Christ (Revelation 20:7-10). The second death is terrifying, which reveals how seriously God takes sin. But if you're a Christian, you have nothing to fear: The second death is not for you.[2]

While it is not necessary to dwell on the horrific details describing the second death, a general understanding of it can cultivate a greater sense of gratitude that motivates us to quickly forgive those who sin against us. In a more positive manner, our desire to forgive others can also be enhanced by reflecting on biblical details of the abundant life that Jesus has saved us for.

JESUS SAVED US FOR AN ABUNDANT LIFE

If the only benefit of salvation were that Jesus saved us from the second death, that would certainly be enough. And yet, because of God's extravagant love and mercy, he has provided us with so much more.

The abundant life is filled with incredible benefits. These include all the aspects of our new identity in Christ and an eternal state of existence that is so wonderful, it is difficult to imagine (1 Corinthians 2:9; 2 Corinthians 12:4). See Appendix B for a partial list of the incredible benefits of our salvation.

As I reflect on the benefits of salvation, I am overwhelmed by God's loving-kindness. I imagine that if I reflected on this list every day and thought regularly about all that is true for me in Christ, I would become more grateful and more eager to forgive others when they sin against me. It would be impossible to hold bitterness in my heart while at the same time being mindful of such a great salvation. My desire to forgive others is directly related to the extent I recognize what Jesus did for me on the cross.

Activated by the Will

The truths of Scripture about the benefits of salvation promote feelings of gratitude, which in turn affect our will—that dynamic of the heart that activates thought and emotion. God commands every Christian to forgive in the same way they have been forgiven (Colossians 3:13); therefore, forgiveness is an act of obedience. But it's also a really good idea, because when we choose to hold on to the hurt caused by an offense, we hurt ourselves.

Unforgiveness creates a stress response in the brain that signals the release of adrenaline and cortisol into the body to prepare us to "fight, flight, or freeze." God designed the body to endure these potent chemicals for a short duration to help us get out of the way or fend off an attack. The body cannot endure a long-term state of stress without doing irreparable harm, however. Caroline Leaf's explanation, quoted earlier in the book, bears repetition here:

> When cortisol and adrenaline are allowed to race unchecked
> through the body, they begin to have adverse effects on the
> cardiovascular system causing high blood pressure, heart
> palpitations and even aneurysms or strokes. They also attack
> the immune system, making it less able to do what it is naturally
> designed to do: protect you from infection and disease. The
> hormones are not yet done on their destructive path. Next, the

cortisol bathes the brain's nerve cells causing memories to literally shrink, affecting the ability to remember and think creatively. This destructive path continues until the body begins to suffer total system breakdown, leading to an emotional black hole, creeping illness and even premature death.[3]

As I nurse a grudge, hold on to an offense, or maintain a victim mindset, feelings of anger, bitterness, and resentment produce a toxic response in my brain, hindering the Christ-formation process and any chance to experience the love, joy, and peace that characterize the abundant life.

Empowered by Grace

As we've discussed, Christ-formation involves our participation, but it is no less driven by the grace of God than any other aspect of our salvation. This is important because forgiveness involves painful memories of bad experiences, which attack our hearts' capacity to choose good.

Fortunately, God works with us in the good work of forgiveness. The Holy Spirit is engaged *with us* in forgiving others. As we reflect on what we know from the Scriptures and tap into our gratitude for the kindness God has extended to us and as we determine to be Christlike in our decisions, we are drawing on God's power to forgive. We are being rewired, becoming both more consistently capable of forgiving and less vulnerable to the destructive work of negative experiences. We are being formed in the image of Christ, and we are moving more steadily toward the abundant life God has in mind for us.

Restoring My Soul with God

In this exercise, I will provide you with a whole-hearted forgiveness process: practical steps to work through specific offenses you have experienced.

1. Write down the name of the person who hurt you.

_____

_____

_____

2. Write down the specific offense using the following questions to guide you:

- How did the offense hurt you? Be specific about the consequences you've experienced as a result.

_____

_____

_____

- How did you react to the offense?

_____

_____

_____

- Did the offense involve other people? If so, who?

_____

_____

_____

3. Write down a passage of Scripture that relates to your experience.

_____

_____

_____

4. Reflect on how, if at all, forgiveness is represented in this Scripture passage. Reflect more generally on what God's forgiveness of your sin has meant for your life.

_____

_____

_____

Share what you wrote with a trusted friend who will give you safe feedback.

5. Write down what will be involved in forgiving the person you identified on page 186.

_____

_____

_____

6. If possible, and if it is safe to do so, verbalize your forgiveness to the person who hurt you. (This can help to restore a broken relationship. However, you can genuinely forgive a person even if that person has died or is otherwise beyond your reach.)

Sometimes, a hurt is so severe that you need to work through all the steps in this process with a trusted friend, pastor, or therapist.

Restoring My Soul with Others

1. Does Ken's story remind you of a time when you were profoundly hurt by others? How did you work through the forgiveness process? Did anyone help you?

2. What details stand out to you from the parable of the unmerciful servant (Matthew 18:21-35)? Discuss.

3. When you consider the great debt of sin that God forgave you for, how does that help you to forgive others who sin against you?

4. Review the benefits of salvation in Appendix B and discuss the specific benefits that stand out to you. How do these stir up gratitude in your heart? Do they help your willingness to forgive others? Why or why not?

5. How does holding on to bitterness and resentment affect you physically?

6. What are the dangers inherent in harboring unforgiveness in your heart?

Conclusion

YOU HAVE BEEN EQUIPPED WITH the knowledge you need to continue to "work out your own salvation" (Philippians 2:12). The extent of your Christ-formation and the degree of the abundant life you experience is now in your hands. The road ahead of us is to become more like Jesus Christ in character and quality of life. And you now have a resource to guide you along the way.

The contents in this book are the result of a lifetime of study and personal experience. They continue to be implemented and refined in my own life as well as in the lives of those I minister to through coaching in discipleship and spiritual direction. I pray that you will act on this material in community with others, because if you do, you will experience greater spiritual/emotional transformation than you ever thought possible and gain a greater experience of the abundant life that Jesus has made available to you. You need companions, a community of friends to journey with; you cannot thrive alone.

I look forward to being part of your journey in the future. Go to the

Institute for Discipleship Training (http://idtministries.com/) for information on my online seminars, YouTube videos, retreats, and podcast.

Let me leave you with the clearest illustration I know of the abundant life that Jesus wants for you to experience both now and into eternity:

> The Lord is my best friend and my shepherd.
> I always have more than enough.
> He offers a resting place for me in his luxurious love.
> His tracks take me to an oasis of peace, the quiet brook of bliss.
> That's where he restores and revives my life.
> He opens before me pathways to God's pleasure
> and leads me along in his footsteps of righteousness
> so that I can bring honor to his name.
> Lord, even when your path takes me through
> the valley of deepest darkness,
> fear will never conquer me, for you already have!
> You remain close to me and lead me through it all the way.
> Your authority is my strength and my peace.
> The comfort of your love takes away my fear.
> I'll never be lonely, for you are near.
> You become my delicious feast
> even when my enemies dare to fight.
> You anoint me with the fragrance of your Holy Spirit;
> you give me all I can drink of you until my heart overflows.
> So why would I fear the future?
> For your goodness and love pursue me all the days of my life.
> Then afterward, when my life is through,
> I'll return to your glorious presence to be forever with you!
>
> PSALM 23:1-6, TPT

Appreciation

I am deeply grateful to a community of friends who have been a constant source of encouragement, feedback, and support throughout the development of this material. Special thanks to Aram and Margie Keith, Steve and Jayne Watts, Steve and Joan Graham, Barry and Sherri Finch, Jim and Helen Steinkamp, Mary Ann Azzolina, Eileen Callahan, Dr. Catherine Hart Weber, Russ and Donna Wertz, Brian and Nancy Hunsaker, Eric and Marie Draper, Terry and Steve Zwick, Greg and Deborah Buckingham, Doug and Eileen Trovato, Rich and Kim Hurst, Bob and Laura Koleas, Chris Bonga, and Jim Lauro. As a community of friends, you are a constant reminder to me and Susan of God's loving presence, protection, and provision.

Thank you, Mike and Linda Hearn, for your friendship and generosity. You allowed me to use your beautiful home for over a year to teach through the early versions of this material.

Thank you, Mike and Carolyn Parkinson, we have been ministry partners these last ten years. You have given me the privilege to share my life and message with hundreds of men through the Trinity Encounter Cohorts.

A special thank you to Dr. Bill Gaultiere, who skillfully guided me—spiritually and emotionally—through a very long, dark night of the soul. And to Larry Warner, my spiritual director, who helped me navigate the often-turbulent waters of local church ministry.

Thank you, Pastor Rick Warren, who was instrumental in my painful transition as a senior pastor into a new ministry role as a discipleship coach. Rick trusted me with coaching the numerous campus pastors at Saddleback Church and around the world with my material. I also want to thank Dr. Lon Solomon, who was influential in the development of my own character during the many years we served together at McLean Bible Church in Washington, DC.

Thank you, Don Pape, friend and publisher, for your decade-long belief in me; you turned the dream of this book into a reality. David Zimmerman is my editor at NavPress. I have marveled at David's grasp of this material and its complexities. Along the way, David provided many helpful insights, was an excellent sounding board, and even talked me off the figurative ledge a couple of times. Thanks, David. Special thanks to Elizabeth Schroll, who served as my copy editor. Her careful attention to detail and wise comments were invaluable!

I am also very grateful to Jan Johnson, who, in the midst of a busy speaking schedule and the pressure of making her own writing deadlines, made time to write the foreword.

Appendix A

"One Another" Commands in the New Testament

"Be devoted to one another in love" (Romans 12:10, NIV).

"Honor one another above yourselves" (Romans 12:10, NIV).

"Live in harmony with one another" (Romans 12:16).

"Accept one another" (Romans 15:7, NIV).

"Instruct one another" (Romans 15:14).

"Greet one another with a holy kiss" (Romans 16:16).

"Agree with one another" (1 Corinthians 1:10, NIV).

"Greet one another with a holy kiss" (1 Corinthians 16:20; 2 Corinthians 13:12).

"Serve one another in love" (Galatians 5:13, NLT).

"Be completely humble and gentle; be patient, bearing with one another in love" (Ephesians 4:2, NIV).

"Be kind and compassionate to one another" (Ephesians 4:32, NIV).

"[Speak] to one another with psalms, hymns, and songs from the Spirit" (Ephesians 5:19, NIV).

"Submit to one another" (Ephesians 5:21, NIV).

"Bear with each other and forgive one another if any of you has a grievance against someone" (Colossians 3:13, NIV).

"Teach and admonish one another" (Colossians 3:16, NIV).

"Encourage one another and build one another up" (1 Thessalonians 5:11).

"Encourage one another daily" (Hebrews 3:13, NIV).

"Spur one another on toward love and good deeds" (Hebrews 10:24, NIV).

"Encourage one another" (Hebrews 10:25, NLT).

"Do not slander one another" (James 4:11, NIV).

"Love one another deeply, from the heart" (1 Peter 1:22, NIV).

"Be like-minded, be sympathetic, love one another, be compassionate and humble" (1 Peter 3:8, NIV).

"Offer hospitality to one another without grumbling" (1 Peter 4:9, NIV).

"Clothe yourselves with humility toward one another" (1 Peter 5:5, NIV).

"Greet one another with the kiss of love" (1 Peter 5:14).

"Love one another" (1 John 3:11; 4:7, 11; 2 John 1:5).

Appendix B

The Benefits of Salvation

God has written my name on the palm of his hand and in the Book of
   Life (Isaiah 49:16; Revelation 20:11-15).

My body is a temple of the Holy Spirit; God's Spirit lives in me
   (1 Corinthians 6:19-20).

I have been ransomed from sin, and I'm free from the law of sin and
   death (Ephesians 1:7; 1 Peter 1:18).

I am no longer a slave to sin (Romans 6:6-7).

Jesus died on the cross to pay my debt for sin in full (John 19:30).

I am clothed in the righteousness of Christ (2 Corinthians 5:21).

Jesus is preparing my home in heaven (John 14:1-4).

I will live with God and his people in the new heaven and earth, where
   there will be no more crying or pain (Revelation 21:1).

I will rule and reign with Christ (Revelation 20:1-6).

I will have a new, glorified body and will live for eternity free from
   pain (1 Corinthians 15:42-53).

I am seated with Christ, right now, in the heavenlies (Ephesians 2:6).

My salvation is secure; it has been sealed by the Holy Spirit
   (Ephesians 1:13-14).

Satan has no power over me (Galatians 2:20; 1 John 4:4).

I can trust God to take care of me in this life and the next
   (Joshua 1:9; Psalm 57:1).

The Holy Spirit gives me strength to live for God (Ephesians 3:16;
   2 Peter 1:3).

I have been created in Christ to do good works during this life (Ephesians 2:10).

God has created me in his image, thereby decreeing my value and worth (Genesis 1:27).

Jesus is my shepherd; he cares for me (Psalm 23; John 10:14-15).

God knows me by name, and he knows all the intimate details of my life (Isaiah 43:1-2; Jeremiah 1:5).

Because God is all-powerful, all-present, all-knowing, and good, there is nothing in this life or the next to fear (Isaiah 41:10, 13; 43:2-3, 5).

The abundant life—a life characterized by love, joy, peace, and hope— is available to me today (John 10:10).

God cares about the things that have hurt me; he has collected every tear in his bottle (Psalm 56:8).

God loves me just as much as he loves Jesus, his only begotten Son (John 17:23).

God is good. He will never abandon me, reject me, betray me, or hurt me in any way (Nahum 1:7; Psalm 34:8).

God will work out everything in my life for my good (Romans 8:28).

Appendix C

My Identity in Christ

The following list is from Neil T. Anderson, *Victory Over the Darkness: Realize the Power of Your Identity in Christ* (Minneapolis: Bethany House, 2013), 51–53.

I am the salt of the earth (Matthew 5:13).

I am the light of the world (Matthew 5:14).

I am a child of God (John 1:12).

I am part of the true vine, a channel of Christ's life (John 15:1, 5).

I am Christ's friend (John 15:15).

I am chosen and appointed by Christ to bear His fruit (John 15:16).

I am a slave of righteousness (Romans 6:18).

I am enslaved to God (Romans 6:22).

I am a son of God; God is spiritually my Father (Romans 8:14-15; Galatians 3:26, 4:6).

I am a joint heir with Christ, sharing His inheritance with Him (Romans 8:17).

I am a temple—a dwelling place—of God. His Spirit and His life dwell in me (1 Corinthians 3:16, 6:19).

I am united to the Lord and am one spirit with Him (1 Corinthians 6:17).

I am a member of Christ's body (1 Corinthians 12:27; Ephesians 5:30).

I am a new creation (2 Corinthians 5:17).

I am reconciled to God and am a minister of reconciliation (2 Corinthians 5:18-19).

I am a son of God and one in Christ (Galatians 3:26, 28).

I am an heir of God since I am a son of God (Galatians 4:6-7).

I am a saint (1 Corinthians 1:2; Ephesians 1:1; Philippians 1:1; Colossians 1:2).

I am God's workmanship—His handiwork—born anew in Christ to do His work (Ephesians 2:10).

I am a fellow citizen with the rest of God's family (Ephesians 2:19).

I am a prisoner of Christ (Ephesians 3:1, 4:1).

I am righteous and holy (Ephesians 4:24).

I am a citizen of heaven, seated in heaven right now (Ephesians 2:6; Philippians 3:20).

I am hidden with Christ in God (Colossians 3:3).

I am an expression of the life of Christ because He is my life (Colossians 3:4).

I am chosen of God, holy and dearly loved (Colossians 3:12; 1 Thessalonians 1:4).

I am a son of light and not of darkness (1 Thessalonians 5:5).

I am a holy partaker of a heavenly calling (Hebrews 3:1).

I am a partaker of Christ; I share in His life (Hebrews 3:14).

I am one of God's living stones, being built up in Christ as a spiritual house (1 Peter 2:5).

I am a member of a chosen race, a royal priesthood, a holy nation, a people for God's own possession (1 Peter 2:9-10).

I am an alien and stranger to this world in which I temporarily live (1 Peter 2:11).

I am an enemy of the devil (1 Peter 5:8).

I am a child of God and I will resemble Christ when He returns (1 John 3:1-2).

I am born of God, and the evil one—the devil—cannot touch me (1 John 5:18).

I am *not* the great "I am" (Exodus 3:14; John 8:24, 28, 58), but by the grace of God, I am what I am (1 Corinthians 15:10).

Appendix D

Standing Firm against Satan

"Submit yourselves therefore to God. Resist the devil, and he will flee from you" (James 4:7).

"Be sober-minded; be watchful. Your adversary the devil prowls around like a roaring lion, seeking someone to devour" (1 Peter 5:8).

"Watch and pray that you may not enter into temptation" (Matthew 26:41).

"No temptation has overtaken you that is not common to man. God is faithful, and he will not let you be tempted beyond your ability, but with the temptation he will also provide the way of escape, that you may be able to endure it" (1 Corinthians 10:13).

"Resist him, firm in your faith, knowing that the same kinds of suffering are being experienced by your brotherhood throughout the world" (1 Peter 5:9).

"Put on the whole armor of God, that you may be able to stand against the schemes of the devil" (Ephesians 6:11).

"Even Satan disguises himself as an angel of light" (2 Corinthians 11:14).

"Jesus was led up by the Spirit into the wilderness to be tempted by the devil" (Matthew 4:1).

"The great dragon was thrown down, that ancient serpent, who is called the devil and Satan, the deceiver of the whole world—he was thrown down to the earth, and his angels were thrown down with him" (Revelation 12:9).

"Lead us not into temptation, but deliver us from evil" (Matthew 6:13).

"I can do all things through him who strengthens me" (Philippians 4:13).

"Because he himself has suffered when tempted, he is able to help those who are being tempted" (Hebrews 2:18).

"Give no opportunity to the devil" (Ephesians 4:27).

"Whoever makes a practice of sinning is of the devil, for the devil has been sinning from the beginning. The reason the Son of God appeared was to destroy the works of the devil" (1 John 3:8).

"Since therefore the children share in flesh and blood, he himself likewise partook of the same things, that through death he might destroy the one who has the power of death, that is, the devil" (Hebrews 2:14).

"The devil who had deceived them was thrown into the lake of fire and sulfur where the beast and the false prophet were, and they will be tormented day and night forever and ever" (Revelation 20:10).

Appendix E

List of Feelings

This table is adapted from Aundi Kolber, *Try Softer: A Fresh Approach to Move Us out of Anxiety, Stress, and Survival Mode—and into a Life of Connection and Joy* (Carol Stream, IL: Tyndale Momentum, 2020), 172, building on the work of Paul Ekman in *Emotion in the Human Face: Guidelines for Research and an Integration of Findings* (Oxford: Pergamon Press, 1972).

HAPPY	SAD	ANGRY	FEARFUL	SURPRISED	DISGUSTED
AMUSED	BLUE	AGITATED	AFRAID	ASTONISHED	CYNICAL
CAREFREE	BURDENED	AGGRAVATED	ALARMED	CONFUSED	DISILLUSIONED
DELIGHTED	DEPRESSED	BITTER	ANTSY	CURIOUS	DISTURBED
EXCITED	DESPONDENT	BROODING	ANXIOUS	DELIGHTED	EMBARRASSED
EXHILARATED	DISAPPOINTED	CRANKY	BROODING	ENCHANTED	EXASPERATED
GIDDY	DISCOURAGED	CROSS	CAUTIOUS	HORRIFIED	FED UP
GRATEFUL	DRAINED	DEFENSIVE	DESPAIRING	INCREDULOUS	HUMILIATED
JOYFUL	GLOOMY	FRUSTRATED	FRIGHTENED	IMPRESSED	JADED
LOVED	GRIEF-STRICKEN	FURIOUS	HELPLESS	INQUISITIVE	JEALOUS
MERRY	HOPELESS	HOSTILE	HESITANT	INTRIGUED	OFFENDED
OPTIMISTIC	LONELY	IMPATIENT	INSECURE	MYSTIFIED	OUTRAGED
RELAXED	MELANCHOLIC	REBELLIOUS	NERVOUS	PUZZLED	REPULSED
SATISFIED	PENSIVE	RESENTFUL	RATTLED	SHOCKED	REVOLTED
THRILLED	REMORSEFUL	SCORNED	STRESSED	SKEPTICAL	SCANDALIZED
TRANQUIL	TROUBLED	TESTY	TENSE	STARTLED	SICKENED
UPBEAT	WEARY	UPSET	WORRIED	WARY	SMUG

Notes

INTRODUCTION

1. I like to make the distinction between "local church" (which is a building) and "the church" as the body of Christ. As believers, we are the church.
2. I'm intentionally writing spiritual/emotional conflicts to read as one to avoid implying they are two separate and unrelated experiences. A spiritual problem promotes an emotional problem and vice versa.
3. The principles and basic premise of this book were first published in my doctoral dissertation: "Emotionally Healthy Discipleship: A Process for Resolving the Spiritual and Emotional Conflicts that Hinder Sanctification" (DMin diss., Biola University, 2016), https://search.proquest.com/openview/73b9d3be7148e65bd47bc2d6927bd3bb/1?pq-origsite=gscholar&cbl=18750&diss=y.

1 DEFINING THE DISCIPLESHIP PROBLEM

1. Willow Creek Community Church, *REVEAL Spiritual Life Survey Technical Report*, July 1, 2015, https://static1.squarespace.com/static/5728d36e4d088eb3ad981105/t/576c67a5ebbd1aee23f5c16f/1466722215020/REVEAL+Spiritual+Life+Survey+Technical+Report+3.0.pdf.
2. Greg L. Hawkins and Cally Parkinson, *Move: What 1,000 Churches Reveal about Spiritual Growth* (Grand Rapids, MI: Zondervan, 2011), 49.

2 THE ABUNDANT LIFE

1. D. A. Carson, *The Gospel According to John*, Pillar New Testament Commentary (Grand Rapids, MI: Eerdmans, 1991), 385.
2. Wilkie Au and Noreen Cannon Au, *God's Unconditional Love: Healing Our Shame* (Mahwah, NJ: Paulist Press, 2016), 11.
3. Craig S. Keener, *The Gospel of John: A Commentary*, vol. 2 (Peabody, MA: Hendrickson, 2003), 1063.
4. See also Isaiah 54:8; Jeremiah 31:3; Romans 8:39.
5. In Appendix D, you will find a list of verses that will help you stand firm against Satan.

3 INGREDIENTS FOR CHRIST-FORMATION
1. I credit the idea of trying versus training to Dallas Willard in *The Spirit of the Disciplines: Understanding How God Changes Lives* (New York: Harper & Row, 1988), 3.
2. See Appendix C for a list explaining your identity in Christ.
3. "Since the 17th century, the scientific method has been the gold standard for investigating the natural world. It is how scientists correctly arrive at new knowledge, and update their previous knowledge. It consists of systematic observation, measurement, experiment, and the formulation of questions or hypotheses." Martyn Shuttleworth and Lyndsay T. Wilson, "What Is the Scientific Method?" Explorable.com, accessed April 10, 2018, https://bit.ly/2GM8Rja.
4. See Appendix A for a list of the "one another" commands in the New Testament.
5. Joseph H. Hellerman, *When the Church Was a Family: Recapturing Jesus' Vision for Authentic Christian Community* (Nashville: B&H Academic, 2009), 31.
6. Richard Plass and James Cofield, *The Relational Soul: Moving from False Self to Deep Connection* (Downers Grove, IL: IVP Books, 2014), 15.
7. Philip Yancey, *What's So Amazing about Grace?* (Grand Rapids, MI: Zondervan, 1997), 45.
8. Dallas Willard, *The Great Omission: Reclaiming Jesus's Essential Teachings on Discipleship* (New York: Harper Collins, 2006), 76.
9. Larry Warner, *Journey with Jesus: Discovering the Spiritual Exercises of Saint Ignatius* (Downers Grove, IL: IVP Books, 2010), 83.

4 THE ABUNDANT LIFE IS A MATTER OF THE HEART
1. The two most common Hebrew words for heart in the Old Testament are *leb* and *lebab*, which are used 858 times. Hans Walter Wolff, *Anthropology of the Old Testament*, trans. Margaret Kohl (London: SCM Press, 1974), chap. V. The most common Greek word in the New Testament is *kardia*, which is used 156 times. Robert Saucy, *Minding the Heart: The Way of Spiritual Transformation* (Grand Rapids, MI: Kregel, 2013), 34.
2. Saucy, *Minding the Heart*, 28. Emphasis in original.
3. Hans Walter Wolff, *Anthropology of the Old Testament*, trans. Margaret Kohl (London: SCM Press, 1974), 46.
4. Dallas Willard, *Renovation of the Heart: Putting on the Character of Christ* (Colorado Springs: NavPress, 2002), 33.
5. E. James Wilder, Anna Kang, John Loppnow, and Sungshim Loppnow, *Joyful Journey: Listening to Immanuel* (Los Angeles: Presence and Practice, 2020), 16.
6. James Bryan Smith, *Hidden in Christ: Living as God's Beloved* (Downers Grove, IL: IVP Books, 2013), 37.
7. David E. Garland, *The NIV Application Commentary: Colossians and Philemon* (Grand Rapids, MI: Zondervan, 1998), 202.

5 SIN AS THE HINDRANCE TO CHRIST-FORMATION
1. Henry Cloud, *Changes That Heal: How to Understand Your Past to Ensure a Healthier Future* (Grand Rapids, MI: Zondervan, 1990), 47.
2. Ibid., 49.
3. Anthony A. Hoekema, *Created in God's Image* (Grand Rapids, MI: Eerdmans, 1986), 76–77.
4. Robert L. Saucy, "Theology of Human Nature," in *Christian Perspectives on Being Human: A Multidisciplinary Approach to Integration*, ed. J. P. Moreland and David M. Ciocchi (Eugene, OR: Wipf & Stock, 2015), 46.

5. Gordon R. Lewis and Bruce A. Demarest, *Integrative Theology* (Grand Rapids, MI: Zondervan, 1996), 208.

6. John Townsend, *Hiding from Love: How to Change the Withdrawal Patterns that Isolate and Imprison You* (Colorado Springs: NavPress, 1991), 66.

7. Henry Cloud and John Townsend, *How People Grow: What the Bible Reveals about Personal Growth* (Grand Rapids, MI: Zondervan, 2001), 122.

6 THE SPIRITUAL/EMOTIONAL CONFLICTS THAT HINDER CHRIST-FORMATION

1. James D. Hamilton, *The Faces of God: How Our Images of God Affect Us* (Kansas City: Beacon Hill Press, 1984), 11–12.

2. Christopher Bader, et al., "American Piety in the 21st Century New Insights to the Depth and Complexity of Religion in the US: Selected Findings from the Baylor Religion Survey," Baylor Institute for Studies of Religion and Department of Sociology, Baylor University, September 2006, https://bit.ly/2Euuoyw.

3. Hamilton, *Faces of God*, 27–28.

4. Ibid., 10.

5. Dallas Willard, *Renovation of the Heart: Putting on the Character of Christ* (Colorado Springs: NavPress, 2002), 13.

6. James W. Sire, *The Universe Next Door: A Basic Worldview Catalog*, 5th ed. (Downers Grove, IL: InterVarsity Press, 2009), 10.

7. You can find out more information about Bill Gaultiere's ministry with his wife, Kristi Gaultiere, at: www.soulshepherding.org.

8. The apostle Peter writes, "God opposes the proud but gives grace to the humble" (1 Peter 5:5-6).

9. You can watch the reconciliation service at: https://www.soulshepherding.org/videos/reconciling-pastor-elder-board/.

10. See, for example, Karl Lehman, *Outsmarting Yourself: Catching Your Past Invading the Present and What to Do about It*, 2nd ed. (Libertyville, IL: This Joy Books, 2014), 97–102. Dr. Karl Lehman, a Christian psychiatrist who works with Jim Wilder, has an excellent discussion about how past unresolved emotions get triggered and brought into the present.

11. Caroline Leaf, *Switch On Your Brain: The Key to Peak Happiness, Thinking, and Health* (Grand Rapids, MI: Baker Books, 2013), 34.

12. Curt Thompson, *The Soul of Shame: Retelling the Stories We Believe about Ourselves* (Downers Grove, IL: IVP Books, 2015), 50.

13. J. P. Moreland, *Love Your God with All Your Mind: The Role of Reason in the Life of the Soul* (Colorado Springs: NavPress, 1997), 73.

7 THE DECEPTIVE POWER OF SHAME

1. For more on healthy shame, see E. James Wilder, *The Pandora Problem: Facing Narcissism in Leaders and Ourselves* (Carmel, IN: Deeper Walk International, 2018).

2. See Jeff Guinn, *Manson: The Life and Times of Charles Manson* (New York: Simon & Schuster, 2013).

3. Brené Brown, *I Thought It Was Just Me (but It Isn't): Making the Journey from "What Will People Think?" to "I Am Enough"* (New York: Gotham Books, 2007), 279.

4. Thomas J. Scheff, "Shame in Self and Society," *Symbolic Interaction* 26, no. 2 (May 2003): 239.

5. Curt Thompson, *The Soul of Shame: Retelling the Stories We Believe about Ourselves* (Downers Grove, IL: IVP Books, 2015), 99.

6. Wilkie Au and Noreen Cannon Au, *God's Unconditional Love: Healing Our Shame* (Mahwah, NJ: Paulist Press, 2016), 11.

7. Brown, *I Thought It Was Just Me*, 20.

8. See, for example, Ethan Kross et al., "Social Rejection Shares Somatosensory Representations with Physical Pain," *Proceedings of the National Academy of Sciences* 108, no. 15 (April 12, 2011), 6270, https://www.pnas.org/content/pnas/108/15/6270 .full.pdf.

9. Caroline Leaf, *Who Switched Off My Brain? Controlling Toxic Thoughts and Emotions* (Southlake, TX: Switch On Your Brain International, 2007), 9–10.

10. Thompson, *Soul of Shame*, 72.

8 HOW NEUROSCIENCE INFORMS CHRIST-FORMATION

1. James E. Zull, "The Art of Changing the Brain," *Educational Leadership* 62, no. 1 (September 2004): 69, accessed June 17, 2016, http://citeseerx.ist.psu.edu/viewdoc /download?doi=10.1.1.504.5667&rep=rep1&type=pdf.

2. Vivian Giang, "Your Brain Is Particularly Vulnerable to Trauma at Two Distinct Ages," *Quartz*, August 4, 2015, https://bit.ly/2qW2Ojy.

3. Caroline Leaf, *Who Switched Off My Brain? Controlling Toxic Thoughts and Emotions* (Southlake, TX: Switch On Your Brain International, 2007), introduction.

4. Joseph H. Hellerman, *When the Church Was a Family: Recapturing Jesus' Vision for Authentic Christian Community* (Nashville: B&H Academic, 2009), 4.

5. For more information on how culture shapes the thinking aspect of the heart, see: Marianna Pogosyan, "How Culture Wires Our Brains," *Psychology Today*, January 26, 2017, https://bit.ly/2T1GjI0.

6. Peter Scazzero with Warren Bird, *The Emotionally Healthy Church: A Strategy for Discipleship That Actually Changes Lives* (Grand Rapids, MI: Zondervan, 2004), 51.

7. A. W. Tozer, *The Knowledge of the Holy* (New York: HarperCollins, 1961), 1–2.

8. Thomas M. Bartol, et al., "Memory Capacity of Brain Is 10 Times More Than Previously Thought," Salk News, January 20, 2016, http://www.salk.edu/news-release/memory -capacity-of-brain-is-10-times-more-than-previously-thought/.

9. Caroline Leaf, *Switch On Your Brain: The Key to Peak Happiness, Thinking, and Health* (Grand Rapids, MI: Baker Books, 2013), 63.

10. Ibid., 20.

11. Bogdan Draganski et al., "Changes in Grey Matter Induced by Training," *Nature* 427, no. 6972 (January 22, 2004), 311–12.

12. Jeffrey M. Schwartz and Rebecca Gladding, *You Are Not Your Brain: The Four-Step Solution for Changing Bad Habits, Ending Unhealthy Thinking, and Taking Control of Your Life* (New York: Penguin Group, 2011), 39–40.

13. Michael S. Gazzaniga, *Who's in Charge? Free Will and the Science of the Brain* (New York: HarperCollins, 2011), 13.

14. Norman Doidge, *The Brain's Way of Healing: Remarkable Discoveries and Recoveries from the Frontiers of Neuroplasticity* (New York: Viking, 2015), 8.

15. Schwartz and Gladding, *You Are Not Your Brain*, 67.

9 BREAKING FREE FROM PAINFUL MEMORIES

1. Moisés Silva, *The Wycliffe Exegetical Commentary: Philippians* (Chicago: Moody Press, 1988), 180.

2. "Bible Concordance: 'Remember,'" LearntheBible.org, accessed August 3, 2020, http://www.learnthebible.org/bible/concordance/19434.

3. Caroline Leaf, *Who Switched Off My Brain? Controlling Toxic Thoughts and Emotions* (Southlake, TX: Switch On Your Brain International, 2007), 27.

4. Daniel J. Siegel, *The Developing Mind: How Relationships and the Brain Interact to Shape Who We Are*, 2nd ed. (New York: Guilford Press, 2012), 39.

5. Caroline Leaf, *Switch On Your Brain: The Key to Peak Happiness, Thinking, and Health* (Grand Rapids, MI: Baker Books, 2013), 123.

6. Robert Saucy, *Minding the Heart: The Way of Spiritual Transformation* (Grand Rapids, MI: Kregel, 2013), 82.

7. Richard O'Connor, *Rewire: Change Your Brain to Break Bad Habits, Overcome Addictions, Conquer Self-Destructive Behavior* (New York: Plume, 2015), 16.

8. Saucy, *Minding the Heart*, 86.

9. Daniel L. Schacter, *Searching for Memory: The Brain, the Mind, and the Past* (New York: Basic Books, 1996), 17.

10. John H. Coe and Todd W. Hall, *Psychology in the Spirit: Contours of a Transformational Psychology* (Downers Grove, IL: IVP Academic, 2010), 238.

11. Leaf, *Who Switched Off My Brain?*, 23.

10 THE TRANSFORMING POWER OF BIBLICALLY INFORMED THINKING

1. John MacArthur, *Romans 9–16*, MacArthur New Testament Commentary (Chicago: Moody, 1994), 150.

2. James D. G. Dunn, *The Epistles to the Colossians and to Philemon: A Commentary on the Greek Text*, New International Greek Testament Commentary (Grand Rapids, MI: Eerdmans, 1996), 205.

3. John MacArthur, *Colossians and Philemon*, MacArthur New Testament Commentary (Chicago: Moody, 1992), 128.

4. Grant R. Osborne, *Philippians: Verse by Verse*, Osborne New Testament Commentaries (Bellingham, WA: Lexham Press, 2017), 176.

5. Robert Saucy, *Minding the Heart: The Way of Spiritual Transformation* (Grand Rapids, MI: Kregel, 2013), 127.

11 THE ROLE OF THE HOLY SPIRIT IN CHRIST-FORMATION

1. Francis Chan, *Forgotten God: Reversing Our Tragic Neglect of the Holy Spirit* (Colorado Springs: David C. Cook, 2009), 16.

2. See also: Romans 8:9, 11; 1 Corinthians 3:16; and 1 John 2:27.

3. Neil T. Anderson and Robert L. Saucy, *God's Power at Work in You: Unleashing the Fullness of God's Power* (Eugene, OR: Harvest House, 2001), 77–78.

4. Of course, Jesus is our "ever-exalted and superior, unique, divine older brother." John Piper, "Jesus Is My Brother—But What Does That Mean?" *Desiring God*, podcast, episode 934, September 7, 2016, https://bit.ly/3fBvj0h.

5. Dallas Willard, *Renovation of the Heart: Putting on the Character of Christ* (Colorado Springs: NavPress, 2002), 13.

6. Karl Lehman, *Outsmarting Yourself: Catching Your Past Invading the Present and What to Do about It*, 2nd ed. (Libertyville, IL: This Joy Books, 2014), 14.

7. Judith Hougen, *Transformed into Fire: An Invitation to Life in the True Self* (Grand Rapids, MI: Kregel Publications, 2002), 23.

8. Ibid., 22.

9. Neil T. Anderson, *Victory over the Darkness: Realize the Power of Your Identity in Christ* (Minneapolis: Bethany House, 2013), 24.

10. E. James Wilder, Anna Kang, John Loppnow, and Sungshim Loppnow, *Joyful Journey: Listening to Immanuel* (Los Angeles: Presence and Practice, 2020), 16.

11. Lehman, *Outsmarting Yourself*, 165.

12. Wilder, Kang, Loppnow, and Loppnow, *Joyful Journey*, 33.

13. Ibid., 22.

12 THE TRANSFORMING POWER OF GOD'S LOVE

1. Earl Henslin, *This Is Your Brain on Joy: How the New Science of Happiness Can Help You Feel Good and Be Happy* (Nashville: Thomas Nelson, 2008), 45.

2. Bruce K. Alexander, "Addiction: The View from Rat Park (2010)," accessed July 10, 2016, http://www.brucekalexander.com/articles-speeches/177-addiction-the-view -from-rat-park-2.

3. James J. Lynch, *The Broken Heart: The Medical Consequences of Loneliness* (New York: Basic Books, 1977), 35.

4. Anthony Walsh, *The Science of Love: Understanding Love and Its Effects on Mind and Body* (Buffalo, NY: Prometheus Books, 1991), 37.

5. Ashley Montagu, *Growing Young* (New York: McGraw-Hill, 1981), 92.

6. John Bowlby, *Attachment and Loss*, vol. 1, *Attachment*, 2nd ed. (New York: Basic Books, 1969), 194.

7. Jude Cassidy, "The Nature of the Child's Ties," in *Handbook of Attachment: Theory, Research, and Clinical Applications*, 2nd ed., ed. Jude Cassidy and Phillip R. Shaver (New York: The Guilford Press, 2008), 3.

8. Amir Levin and Rachel S. F. Heller, *Attached: The New Science of Adult Attachment and How It Can Help You Find—and Keep—Love* (New York: TarcherPerigee, 2011), 12.

9. Harry F. Harlow and Stephen J. Suomi, "Social Recovery by Isolation-Reared Monkeys," *Proceedings of the National Academy of Sciences Journal* 68, no. 7 (July 1971): 1534, https://www.ncbi.nlm.nih.gov/pmc/articles/PMC389234/pdf/pnas00082-0155.pdf.

10. The Beatles, "All You Need Is Love," *All You Need Is Love* (single) © 1967 Parlophone, 45 rpm.

11. Douglas J. Moo, *The Epistle to the Romans*, The New International Commentary on the New Testament (Grand Rapids, MI: Eerdmans, 1996), 305.

12. D. A. Carson, *The Gospel According to John*, Pillar New Testament Commentary (Grand Rapids, MI: Eerdmans, 1991), 517.

13. A fun fact is that we actually have seven senses: sight, smell, taste, hearing, touch, *vestibular*, and *proprioception*. For more information, see: http://www.7senses.org .au/what-are-the-7-senses/.

14. Sandy Fritz and Luke Fritz, *Mosby's Essential Sciences for Therapeutic Massage: Anatomy, Physiology, Biomechanics, and Pathology*, 6th ed. (St. Louis: Elsevier, 2021), 583.

15. Harold W. Hoehner, *Ephesians: An Exegetical Commentary* (Grand Rapids, MI: Baker Academic, 2002), 488–489.

16. Craig S. Keener, *The Gospel of John: A Commentary*, vol. 2 (Peabody, MA: Hendrickson, 2003), 1063.

17. Carson, *The Gospel According to John*, 569. Emphasis mine.

18. Roger Carswell, "Henry Moorhouse," *Evangelical Times*, August 2018, https://www .evangelical-times.org/43935/henry-moorhouse/.

19. John Pollock, *D. L. Moody: Moody without Sankey* (Ross-shire, Great Britain: Christian Focus Publications, 2005), 113.

20. Name has been changed to protect his identity.

21. Curt Thompson, *Anatomy of the Soul: Surprising Connections between Neuroscience and Spiritual Practices That Can Transform Your Life and Relationships* (Carol Stream, IL: SaltRiver Books, 2010), 77.

22. Milan and Kay Yerkovich, *How We Love: Discover Your Love Style, Enhance Your Marriage* (Colorado Springs: WaterBrook, 2017).

13 SPIRITUAL DISCIPLINES TO REWIRE YOUR BRAIN

1. John MacArthur, *2 Corinthians*, MacArthur New Testament Commentary (Chicago: Moody Press, 2003), 329.

2. Dallas Willard, *The Great Omission: Reclaiming Jesus's Essential Teachings on Discipleship* (New York: HarperSanFrancisco, 2006), 105.

3. The total number of words differs depending on which translation you are reading.

4. Robert Saucy, *Minding the Heart: The Way of Spiritual Transformation* (Grand Rapids, MI: Kregel, 2013), 134.

5. Eugene H. Peterson, *Eat This Book: A Conversation in the Art of Spiritual Reading* (Grand Rapids: MI: Eerdmans, 2006), 59.

6. Wayne Grudem, *Systematic Theology: An Introduction to Biblical Doctrine* (Grand Rapids, MI: Zondervan, 1994), 180.

7. Allyson Holland, "10 Names of God and What They Mean," Crosswalk.com, April 23, 2018, https://bit.ly/2H4dV3D.

8. I am indebted to Dr. Neil Anderson, who has helped shape my understanding of my identity in Christ.

9. Neil T. Anderson, *Victory over the Darkness: Realize the Power of Your Identity in Christ* (Minneapolis: Bethany House, 2013), 47.

10. Saucy, *Minding the Heart*, 153.

11. James W. Goll, *The Lost Art of Practicing His Presence* (Shippensburg, PA: Destiny Image, 2005), 132.

12. Edward M. Curtis and John J. Brugaletta, *Discovering the Way of Wisdom: Spirituality in the Wisdom Literature* (Grand Rapids, MI: Kregel, 2004), 165.

13. Dallas Willard, "Spiritual Formation in Christ for the Whole Life and Whole Person," *Vocatio* 12, no. 2 (Spring 2001): 7.

14. I recommend *Chegg Flashcards+* by Chegg Inc. (https://che.gg/2j7uqhJ) and *The Bible Memory App* by Millennial Apps, LLC (https://biblememory.com). Both are available for Apple and Android phones.

15. Warren W. Wiersbe, *BE Complete: NT Commentary, Colossians* (Colorado Springs: David C. Cook, 1981).

16. James Bryan Smith, *Hidden in Christ: Living as God's Beloved* (Downers Grove, IL: IVP Books, 2013).

14 SPIRITUAL DISCIPLINES TO HEAL THE HEART
1. Henri J. M. Nouwen, *The Way of the Heart* (New York: Random House, 1981), 15.
2. Adele Ahlberg Calhoun, *Spiritual Disciplines Handbook: Practices that Transform Us* (Downers Grove, IL: IVP Books, 2005), 112–13.
3. D. Edmond Hiebert, *The Epistle of James: Tests of a Living Faith* (Chicago: Moody, 1979), 316–17.
4. John F. Walvoord and Roy B. Zuck, eds., Dallas Theological Seminary, *The Bible Knowledge Commentary: An Exposition of the Scriptures* (Wheaton, IL: Victor Books, 1985), 835.

15 THE ROLE OF FORGIVENESS IN CHRIST-FORMATION
1. Here is an excellent resource to help you understand pastoral burnout: Bill Gaultiere, "Pastor Stress Statistics," *Soul Shepherding* (blog), accessed May 15, 2020, https://www.soulshepherding.org/pastors-under-stress/.
2. See 1 John 5:4-5 and Revelation 2:11. Every believer is an overcomer and will not experience the second death.
3. Caroline Leaf, *Who Switched Off My Brain? Controlling Toxic Thoughts and Emotions* (Southlake, TX: Switch On Your Brain International, 2007), 9–10.

THE NAVIGATORS® STORY

T HANK YOU for picking up this NavPress book! I hope it has been a blessing to you.

NavPress is a ministry of The Navigators. The Navigators began in the 1930s, when a young California lumberyard worker named Dawson Trotman was impacted by basic discipleship principles and felt called to teach those principles to others. He saw this mission as an echo of 2 Timothy 2:2: "And the things you have heard me say in the presence of many witnesses entrust to reliable people who will also be qualified to teach others" (NIV).

In 1933, Trotman and his friends began discipling members of the US Navy. By the end of World War II, thousands of men on ships and bases around the world were learning the principles of spiritual multiplication by the intentional, person-to-person teaching of God's Word.

After World War II, The Navigators expanded its relational ministry to include college campuses; local churches; the Glen Eyrie Conference Center and Eagle Lake Camps in Colorado Springs, Colorado; and neighborhood and citywide initiatives across the country and around the world.

Today, with more than 2,600 US staff members—and local ministries in more than 100 countries—The Navigators continues the transformational process of making disciples who make more disciples, advancing the Kingdom of God in a world that desperately needs the hope and salvation of Jesus Christ and the encouragement to grow deeper in relationship with Him.

NAVPRESS was created in 1975 to advance the calling of The Navigators by bringing biblically rooted and culturally relevant products to people who want to know and love Christ more deeply. In January 2014, NavPress entered an alliance with Tyndale House Publishers to strengthen and better position our rich content for the future. Through *THE MESSAGE* Bible and other resources, NavPress seeks to bring positive spiritual movement to people's lives.

If you're interested in learning more or becoming involved with The Navigators, go to www.navigators.org. For more discipleship content from The Navigators and NavPress authors, visit www.thedisciplemaker.org. May God bless you in your walk with Him!

www.navpress.com

CP1308